Metaverse For Beginners 2023

The Ultimate Guide on Investing In Metaverse, Blockchain Gaming, Virtual Lands, Augmented Reality, Virtual Reality, NFT, Real Estate, Crypto And Web 3.0

Introduction

Imagine a world where you can virtually be present at a wedding in San Francisco while you're sipping a cup of coffee in Moscow? Or a society where interacting with people is not limited to just blurry video calls and glitchy computer service.

These are the things the metaverse, the next generation of the web, intends to do. But exactly, what is this metaverse? What sets it apart from the rest of the Internet?

A Metaverse is a place where you can interact with virtual items in real-time and with real-time information. In films and shows like Iron Man, Ready Player One, Upload, and The Feed, you've probably already seen this concept being put into practice.

The Metaverse consists of three distinct components. It is first and foremost a technology that allows digital content to be placed on top of the real-world environment. In a way, this is like augmented reality (AR). Using Pokémon Go as a simplistic example, this technology can be improved in future iterations of a metaverse. It's a mix of the digital and real-world stuff. It also uses a hardware gadget to make the natural environment interactive. Using digital material, users can manipulate and interact with media displayed online. The last point includes information on anything and everything in the real world (such as an area, a shop, or a product), along with information about the user (such as the user's timetable). This data will be gleaned through the Internet and machines trained to pick up on users' habits. There are many examples of devices learning from their users' daily behaviors, like Siri (iOS) and Alexa (Android) (on Amazon).

A user's experience is enhanced by obtaining real-time information instantly and virtually through the device into the physical space. At the same time, data is being collected and applied in the background.

To better grasp the Metaverse, one can extrapolate real-world traits to an entirely virtual setting. A metaverse environment will incorporate elements of the actual world into a virtual one. A virtual London or New York, for example, may provide digital representations of real-life streets and buildings to gamers playing in a virtual gaming environment. In a virtual Apple store, you may look through and purchase digital representations of Apple products that will be shipped to your home.

This would, in many ways, represent a continuation of what we currently know as traditional e-commerce. Companies may construct metaverse worlds that not only duplicate the real-life experience but also enhance it, thanks to advances in visual technology and design capability enabled by sophisticated gaming engines like Unreal or Unity. There may be no crowd outside the Manhattan Apple store's digital counterpart at launch time.

The concept of simulating real-world settings in a virtual one is nothing new. It has been going on for a long time with concepts like second life. On the other hand, contemporary online gaming settings have shifted the Metaverse from the old-school 3D block-based worlds of the turn of the century to new, ever-evolving creative ecosystems.

User-created content is the critical difference between the metaverses of the past and today. Playing online games like Fortnite, Roblox, and Minecraft has altered our perceptions of what it means to be "online." When parents wonder why their children spend so much time in these metaverse worlds, it's not because the games or items are well-designed.

Instead, they argue that the metaverses are so compelling and well-designed in and of themselves. People participate, create, and amuse each other rather than just sitting back and watching others. People are paid to make virtual goods in Minecraft, and entire mini-industries have sprung up around them. Fortnite is a virtual stage for real-world music performers to showcase their talents. Every year, tens of millions of people participate in activities that could only occur in the Metaverse.

1. How the Metaverse Works

Several key attributes of the metaverse are revealed by these descriptions. First of all, it will involve entering cyberspace. We will do so by using a headset such as the Oculus. Once we put our headsets on, countless universes will be at our disposal. The nature of the metaverse is still unclear since we do not know if it will be a single metaverse or a collection of multiverses. At the moment, big names in the tech industry are all working on their version of the metaverse. The most likely scenario is that users will decide which ones will become popular.

Once we enter the metaverse of our choice, virtual and augmented reality will take over. We will enter this cyberspace through an avatar. An avatar can be a representation of you or something entirely different. In either case, we can customize this avatar in any way we want. The avatar is your gateway to interacting with the virtual world. This virtual world can be anything from a classroom to moon travel. The possibilities are only limited by imagination. User-generated metaverses won't be a hot topic for the foreseeable future. However, companies that **are** creating the metaverse will surely come up with amazing concepts.

These virtual worlds will have rules of their own. Mark Zuckerberg is one of the people constantly bringing this subject up. Facebook, or Meta as it's now known, seems to have learned from its unpleasant experience with the government a few years ago. Leaving old habits, they tackle privacy, safety, and ethics with a new perspective. To ensure the metaverse is exploit-free, international NGOs have been working with the company since the beginning. In addition, Mark Zuckerberg touched on the topic in an open letter and expressed how important it is for him to create a metaverse where users are free to make their own rules. We have seen a similar approach in Web 2.0. You can befriend, unfriend, and block other users on Facebook, Slack channels are invitation-only, and your Instagram account can be private if you want. The metaverse is expected to provide all this but incorporate more policies to improve safety measures. As a result, we might not influence a metaverse, but we will control how we interact with it.

Finally, metaverses are likely to have their own economies and, in some cases, their own currencies. Metaverse transactions are expected to be made on blockchains, making cryptocurrencies and altcoins ideal tender mediums. With metaverse currencies, we will be able to rent a house, buy concert tickets, go on vacation, and pay for an online course. In addition to bringing cryptocurrencies to a whole new level, many business ideas will be generated through this system.

Right now, aside from a few examples like Decentraland, we don’t have all too many real-life examples of metaverses. However, we do have some fictional examples that can be used to make the metaverse more tangible in our minds.

Metaverse in Pop Culture

Metaverses have existed as fictional concepts for decades. In fact, people like Elon Musk, Mark Zuckerberg, and other influential tech entrepreneurs are all fans of these metaverses. As software creators today, it's not uncommon for them to discuss their love of a particular franchise or book in speeches or interviews.

Star Trek, without a doubt, is one such franchise. Creator Gene Roddenberry always wowed the viewers with his vision of a better, more humane future. This is especially true for **Star Trek: The Next Generation** holodecks. Holodecks appeared in classic **Star Trek** episodes as well, but the holodeck episodes of **Star Trek: The Next Generation** are a perfect example of an early metaverse. An example of a more futuristic metaverse would be the unforgettable **Inner Light** episode. The episode depicts Captain Jean-Luc Picard living an alternate life in a capsule, only to wake up on the USS Enterprise to realize it was just an alternate life. The episode is a fan favorite, so if you're into the metaverse, you will definitely want to watch it.

The Netflix show **Black Mirror** would be a more contemporary example. The show follows a dystopian future of the metaverse, but the concepts implemented are very relevant to the core idea. Another streaming platform series about the metaverse is the Amazon Original **Upload**. Philosophical satire certainly characterizes the series, but it also explores what happens in a dystopia of free-to-play games and the current online world.

If you like fictional dystopias, a good movie depicting the metaverse is **Ready Player One**. The movie does a stellar job demonstrating how VR experiences could be in the future. Another movie that does a decent job with the mechanical side of the metaverse is **Minority Report**. Watching Tom Cruise in his prime aside, holographic images and interfaces coupled with special gloves are excellent examples of how we will navigate in the metaverse.

Another movie that is regularly brought up about the metaverse is Ironman. Tony Stark, the main character in the movie, is essentially forced to create a metaverse. He manages to create both virtual and augmented reality in the movie, which is a remarkable accomplishment and makes for a great film.

One of the best examples of how metaverses could improve the common household is **Smart House**. Our houses are already getting smart. With smart appliances connecting to devices like Alexa, we are already experiencing a tech revolution in our homes. The movie **Smart House** is an excellent example of this, delving deeply into the issue of human vs. technology, while still being entertaining.

These concepts would not exist without the development of technology. Enjoying entertainment centered around the metaverse and imagining its possibilities is both inspiring and fun. But to truly grasp the magic of the metaverse, we need to dig deep into its technological aspects. Let's examine the evolution of the internet and how we got to where we are today.

The Evolution of the Web

Tim Berners-Lee invented the 'web,' as we know it, in Switzerland in the early 1990s. We wouldn't have internet browsers until nearly half a decade later. Several years later, search engines such as Google were invented. Since then, the web and internet technologies have undergone drastic changes. Nowadays, internet use has become a survival tool for millions. There have been three major stages in the history of the internet.

The Static Web

Initially, content on the internet was predetermined. Therefore, people used the term "static web" to describe it. The concept of static content refers to any content that can be delivered to an end-user without having to be generated, modified, or processed. You could make a website, and people could browse it, but they couldn't interact with it beyond leaving a comment.

The main difference between mainstream media and Web 1.0. is user involvement in content consumption. Our lives have been forever changed by the internet because it decentralized content production. Until the internet, only a few media outlets created information, which was consumed by the masses. Having access to the internet meant that everyone could produce content. Moreover, users could influence content creation by not giving attention to the information they did not enjoy. Because of this, Web 1.0 is celebrated as the democratization of information.

Understanding the decentralization of content production is very important. This mindset later led to the decentralization of currencies and gave rise to new technologies such as Bitcoin. In other words, if you wish to achieve anything in the metaverse, just keep in mind that this internet principle always determines success in online businesses.

The Interactive Web

The democratization and decentralization of the internet eventually led to Web 2.0. In this era, people were not limited to consuming content or throwing their two cents in the comment section. With Web 2.0, they could be content creators. Wikipedia, YouTube, WordPress, and Blogger are all examples of Web 2.0's impact on the world.

Web 2.0 had a rough start with the "dot-com bubble." The dot-com bubble was a rapid increase in U.S. technology stock valuations in the late 1990s caused by investments in Web-based companies. The bubble burst in 2001, leaving Nasqad with a 77% drop and investors in a panic. Several web companies collapsed, and, for a moment, it looked like the Web was just a fad.

Obviously, this wasn't the case. Technology was advancing and growing just fine. It was the stock markets that were the problem. Amazon's Jeff Bezos is a perfect example of this. Even though Amazon lost 90% of its value during the bubble, it made its shareholders extremely wealthy, including Bezos, one of the most affluent people in the world. If a scenario like this occurs in the metaverse era, remember one thing: Long-term investors will win out as long as technology is expanding.

As a result of Web 2.0, the internet has become a sea of user-generated content. Sharing information and connecting with others has become the norm. It led to hundreds of thousands of online shops, content creation platforms, and the influencer era.

The Semantic Web

Web 3.0 is predicted to be known as the Semantic Web because it will become more intuitive for every user. The name was coined by none other than Web's original creator Tim Berners-Lee. Scientific American magazine published an article in 2001 in which Bernes-Lee outlined his vision for the internet. As an example, he presented two brothers who coordinate the logistics involved in supporting their mother's medical treatment; using intelligent agents, they execute the process automatically interacting with clinical systems, among themselves, and with their home devices.

This is the kind of intuitive technology we can expect from Web 3.0. In this third generation of the web, the goal is to provide users with a personalized experience based on their interests and needs. Amazon’s Alexa, which collects information from the web and tailors it to our needs, is a prime example of Web 3.0 technologies.

Currently, we're transitioning from Web 2.0 to Web 3.0. We can expect Web 3.0 to have as significant an impact as Web 2.0 has. Web 3.0 will introduce us to many exciting new technologies, including the metaverse. In order to gain a deeper understanding of the metaverse, let's examine some of its key concepts.

2. Virtual Reality (VR)

It is now possible for even the average user to access the world of computer graphics. This obsession with a new reality frequently begins with computer games and continues indefinitely. It allows you to perceive the world around you differently and experience things that aren't available in real life or even haven't been developed yet. Furthermore, the universe of three-dimensional graphics has no boundaries or limitations. We may create and alter it as we see fit—we can even add a fourth dimension: the measurement of our imagination. But it's never enough: people are always looking for more. Instead of just watching a visual on a monitor, they want to enter this world and engage with it. Virtual Reality is a technology that has become extremely popular and fashionable in the last decade (VR). Virtual Reality is thought to have started in the 1950s, although it was only widely used in the late 1980s and 1990s. This might be attributed to Jaron Lanier, a pioneering computer scientist with the term "virtual reality" in 1987. Virtual reality research continued throughout the 1990s, and films like The Lawnmower Man served to enhance its profile. Most virtual reality settings are primarily visual experiences displayed on a computer screen or through stereoscopic displays. Auditory stimulation via speakers or headphones may be included in virtual Reality. The virtual Environment can be interacted with using a keyboard, mouse, or wired glove. Virtual Reality's history has been chiefly one of the attempts to make an experience more authentic. Visual and, to a lesser extent, auditory examples make up the majority of historical examples. This is because vision, followed by hearing, delivers the most information of all the human senses. Visual and auditory perceptions account for roughly 90% of our overall worldview.

Evolution of Virtual Reality (VR)

Ivan Sutherland created the "make (virtual) world phrase in the original window, sounds authentic, feels real, and responds realistically to viewers' activities in 1965. It's been a long time, and many studies have been done since then. Let's peek shortly in the last three decades of study in virtual Reality and its highlights:

« **Sensorama** –The Sensorama engine was founded in 1957 and patented in 1962 under patent # 3,050,870. Morton Heilig creates a multi-sensory simulator. Films that have been recorded in color and stereo coupled with binaural sound, aroma, wind, and vibration. This is the first approach to creating a virtual reality system and has all the features like that, but it's not interactive.

« **Display Ultimate** - in 1965, Ivan Sutherland suggested a central virtual reality solution: an artificial world construction concept that included interactive graphics, force-feedback, sound, smell, and taste.

« Damocles Sword - First Virtual Reality system is realized in hardware, not the concept. Ivan Sutherland builds a device that is considered the first appearance of the head installed (HMD), with the appropriate head tracking. It supports stereo views that are updated correctly according to the position and orientation of the user's head.

What is Virtual Reality (VR)?

The development of virtual Reality extended considerably stormier towards the 1990s, and the term "virtual reality" became extremely widespread. Virtual Reality is a term that we hear about in almost every kind of media; people use it frequently and, in many situations, incorrectly. Virtual Reality (VR) is a popular term for an immersive, interactive computer-mediated experience in which a person observes a synthetic (simulated) environment using specialized human-computer interface equipment.

It interacts with the Environment's virtual objects as if they were real. In a shared synthetic environment, like a battlefield, multiple people can see and interact with one another. A computer-generated virtual environment that a person can move through and change in real-time is called "virtual reality." The virtual Environment can be seen in the display installed in the head, computer monitor, or a large projection screen. Using head and hand tracking devices, the user can see, move about, and alter the Virtual Environment. The significant distinction between VR systems and traditional media (such as radio and television) is the virtual reality structure's three-dimensionality.

Immersion, presence, and interactivity are typical features of virtual Reality which keeps him away from other representational technology. Virtual Reality does not mimic actual Reality also does not have representative functions. Humans cannot distinguish between perceptions, hallucinations, and illusions. VR has developed into a new phase and has become a different field in computing. The VR utility has been studied in car design, robot design, chemistry, biology, education, building design and construction.

Types of Virtual Reality Systems

There are various types of virtual reality systems:

Ø Immersive system.

The highest priority is given to the immersive system. As we have mentioned, the immersive design ruled out the natural world and put humans in the world of animation that was entirely generated by the computer.

Ø Window on World (WoW)

This is a typical virtual world developed on a desktop PC. The most common form of WOW is a computer game that uses real-world 3D simulations. Here users must peek into the virtual world using a monitor placed on the desktop.

Ø Video Mapping

This is a technique used to map human movements using special electronic devices such as cameras. Here input to the computer is a human movement, and output is a human 2D graphics image that shows its interests.

Ø **Telepresence**

This is another virtual reality technique where we use some remote sensors somewhere in the virtual world that maps human actions and connects them to activities that objects in the virtual world must do. Firefighters use this type of virtual reality in several critical conditions. Unique robots that are fixed with this type of sensor help them.

Ø Mixed Reality

This is a technique that combines the system of virtual reality and telepresence. Here the input for the telepresence system and virtual Reality is given information. The fighters see the map produced by the computer and connect it to the data available with it. The surgeon correlates images taken by cat scanning and taken by the computer.

Basic Terminology and Definitions

Many people, mainly the researchers, use the word natural Environment instead of virtual reality "because of the hype and unrealistic expectations related." In addition, two essential terms must be mentioned when talking about VR: telepresence and cyberspace. They are both combined with VRs, but have a slightly different context:

- **Telepresence** – This term was created by Marvin Minsky (1980), referring to the teleoperation system for the manipulation of long-distance physical objects. This is a specific type of virtual reality that simulates a natural but long-distance environment (within a distance or scale or scale). More appropriate definitions say that telepresence occurs when "on the work site, the manipulator has the dexterity to allow operators to perform normal human functions; at the control, stationworksiterator accepts sufficient quantity and the quality of sensory feedback to provide a feeling of actual presence at work."

- **Cyberspace** –Created and defined by William Gibson as "consensual hallucinations experienced every day by billions of valid operators, graphic representations of data witnessed from each computer in the human system." Today the term virtual world is somewhat related to the entertainment system and the World Wide Web (Internet).
- **Telexistence:** This theory was first proposed by Susumu Tachi in Japan in 1980 and 1981 as a patent, and the first report was published in Japanese in 1982 and English in 1984. It allows humans to have a real-time sensation in places besides Where it exists and can interact with a distant environment, which may be accurate, virtual, or a combination of both. It also refers to the sophisticated teleoperation system that allows operators to perform small tasks with feelings in replacement robots that work in a distant environment.

- **Human-Computer Interaction (HCL)** refers to the study and processes humans interact with computers. Very basic HCI is simple like a keyboard and mouse, while HCI is sophisticated can be considered a controlled interaction between someone and a laptop. **Haptics** – The word "haptics" refers to the ability to feel a natural or synthetic mechanical environment through touch. Haptics also include Kinesthesia, the ability to understand body position, movement, and weight. • Haptics technology - provides forced feedback to users about the physical properties and movement of virtual objects represented by computers. A haptic joystick, For example, offers dynamic resistance to users based on video game actions. Haptics combines touch elements (tactile) and movement (kinesthetic). Applications that simulate physical properties such as weight, momentum, friction, texture, or haptics resistance communicate these properties through the interface, allowing users to "feel" what happens on the screen. Immersion Levels in Virtual Reality Systems

A computer generates sensory impressions given to the human senses in a virtual environment system. In Virtual Reality, the type and quality of these perceptions impact the amount of immersion and sense of presence. Ideally, information should be given to all users' minds in high-resolution, high-quality, and consistent across all screens. Furthermore, the Environment should respond realistically to the user's activities. On the other hand, the reality is significantly different from this ideal scenario. Many applications simply stimulate one or a few senses, and they frequently provide low-quality, unsynchronized data. We may categorize VR systems based on the level of immersion they provide to the user.

- **Non-Immersive (Desktop VR) systems** – Virtual desktop reality is a lower immersive level that can be easily used in many applications without special devices. Sometimes it is called a window system in the world (WOW). This is the type of most straightforward virtual reality application. VR Desktop is when computer users see a virtual environment via one or more computer screens. A user can then link with that Environment, but it is not immersed. It uses a conventional monitor to display images (generally monoscopic) in the world. There are no other sensory outputs supported. Virtual Desktop reality has begun to make its way and popularity in modern education because it provides visualization and real-time interaction in the virtual world that resembles the real world.
- **Semi-Immersive (Fish Tank VR) systems** –Enhanced VR Desktop version. This system supports head tracking and therefore increases the feeling of "being there" thanks to the effect of movement parallax. They still use conventional monitors (often with LCD shutter glasses to watch stereoscopic) but generally do not support sensory output.

- **Immersive systems** – The main version of the VR system. They let users immerse themselves in the world produced by a computer with HMD assistance that supports stereoscopic views of the scene according to the position and user orientation. This system can be increased by audio, haptic, and sensory interfaces.

Characteristics of Immersive (VR)

1) The unique characteristics of immersive virtual realities can be summarized as follows: The appearance referenced by the head provides a natural interface for navigation in three-dimensional space and allows one to look, take a walk, and the ability to fly in a virtual environment.
2) Stereoscopic viewing promotes the perception of depth and the sense of space.
3) The virtual world is presented fully and is related to human size.
4) Realistic interactions with virtual objects through data gloves and similar devices allow manipulation, operation, and virtual world control.
5) Convincing illusions to be wholly immersed in the artificial world can be increased by auditories, haptic, and other non-visual technology.
6) Networked applications allow for shared virtual environments.

v Uses of Virtual Reality

It's difficult to define all VR applications because they have advanced far enough in numerous fields. However, some of the applications of virtual Reality are discussed below. Virtual reality software bundle EDS Jack is an example of commercially accessible virtual reality software. It is mainly utilized for research into visibility and ergonomics. These are two of the many areas where Virtual Reality may help. For example, operators value visibility and ergonomics when constructing massive mechanical equipment like a bulldozer or even an automobile.

Probably not. Would you buy a car that was difficult to drive or had poor visibility? Many businesses spend a significant amount of money improving how their products interact with operators. Building prototypes is quite expensive, costing upwards of a few million dollars for single equipment in the case of the bulldozer. The corporation could immediately examine the viability and ergonomics of their machine using virtual Reality and make modifications without ever having to spend money on developing hardware. Driving and flying simulations are other areas where Virtual Reality is widely employed. This allows users to experience driving a car while avoiding real-world punishment to make mistakes. For instance, MPI Vega Prime is a software program that can simulate any form of bullying. Within the software package, the user creates the virtual Environment. Its most significant benefit is its realistic physics engine, which allows collision detection. The most popular sort of machine simulation is flight simulators. Other instances include the employment of simulators by the US Army to train tank soldiers in virtual tank battles. NASA also uses a virtual reality simulator to instruct astronauts on land the space shuttle.

Ø Advantages

Virtual Reality has also been utilized extensively to treat phobias (such as fear of height, fly, and spider) and post-traumatic stress disorders. This kind of therapy has proven effective in academic settings, and some commercial entities now offer them to patients. Although it was found that using a standardized patient for the training was more realistic, computer-based simulations provide several advantages over direct training. They aim to increase exposure to emergencies such as life to improve decision-making and performance and reduce psychological pressure in real health emergencies.

Ø Disadvantages

Some psychologists are worried that immersion in a virtual psychological environment can affect users. They suggest that refreshing the system that places users in a situation of violence, especially as a participant in violence, can lead to users being sensitive. As a result, there is a panic that entertainment systems can breed a sociopath generation. Involving a virtual environment has the potential to make addicted more. Another emergence of concerns involves criminal acts. Defining actions such as murder or sex crimes have been problematic in the virtual world. At which point can the authorities impose a person's fees with real crimes for actions in the virtual Environment? Studies show that people can have a natural physical and emotional reaction to stimulation in the virtual Environment, so it is possible that victims of virtual attacks can feel real emotional trauma.

3. Augmented Reality

While virtual reality is an exclusively digital environment created by one or more computers or applications that simulate actual reality, augmented reality (AR) represents the real world enriched with virtual objects or details that lead to improving or "increasing" the experience.

It is based on the expansion or integration of the surrounding reality with computer-generated 3D graphics images, which modify the original environment without affecting interaction possibilities.

In essence, augmented reality transforms vast masses of data and analytics into images or animations, a digital level that is superimposed on the physical world by integrating with it.

What Does It Take To Create Augmented Reality?

Not being as immersive as virtual reality, it does not necessarily need specific viewers for which everyday devices such as smartphones or special screens can be used (as in the case of car accessories).

How Does Augmented Reality Work?

Augmented reality starts from a device equipped with a video camera - such as a smartphone, tablet, or smart glass - on which AR software has been loaded. When the user indicates the device at an object and looks at it, the software recognizes it through computerized vision technology, which analyzes the flow of images.

Then the device downloads the object information from the cloud, just like a browser downloads a page via the URL. The critical difference is that AR information is presented in a 3D experience superimposed on the object rather than on a two-dimensional page that appears on a screen.

What the user sees, therefore, is partly natural and partly digital. At this point, we must introduce the overlay principle: the camera reads the object in the frame, the system recognizes it. It activates a new level of communication that overlaps and integrates perfectly with reality, enhancing detailed data about that object.

Headsets are the critical technology for both virtual and augmented reality. It is, thus, not unexpected that some of the best-known names in the traditional IT market have thrown themselves into the construction of this equipment which, depending on the model, can be destined for different types of uses (gaming and more).

Google Glass is a trademark of smart glasses developed by the Mountain View company, a pair of glasses equipped with augmented reality through which you can access various information:

you can read websites and news online, check social networks, view maps and driving directions through Google Maps, participate in video conferences, take photos and shoot videos, all without the use of hands (hands-free). Perhaps due to the too-high price, probably because it arrived too early (with the official debut in mid-2014), Google Glass had a reasonably tepid welcome from ordinary consumers, also for issues related to usability, as well as protection of privacy. Google, therefore, withdrew the product from sale, which - despite some relaunch rumors - has never seen the light again.

Augmented And Virtual Reality Viewers

The Oculus Rift, produced by the company of the same name then acquired by Facebook, which, starting from 2016, has quickly established itself as one of the most popular virtual reality viewers for gaming, has been decidedly more fortunate. To contend with the priority, there are other viewers produced by names such as Samsung (with its Gear VR), which needs the latest generation smartphone to work and which is to be inserted inside the mask of the viewer, and Huawei with VR2 (first model released in 2016 and then updated in 2018) which can be connected to a PC to use it with games designed for machines with higher computing power than the integrated one.

Mixed Reality Viewer

In the business field, however, at least for the moment, Microsoft's Hololens (created in 2015 and updated in 2019) has captured the most interest, a viewer for mixed reality, specifically designed to bring value to enterprise projects, i.e., in all those work processes that can benefit from a minimum of digital interaction and in which there is a need to experiment with something new.

Growth Market With Ar In The Lead

The global VR and AR market reached a value of $6.158 billion in 2017 and is expected to travel at a growth rate of 58.1% between now and 2023. The growing penetration of smartphones, along with advances, will drive the market in connectivity and information technology, in addition to the significant investments and innovations conducted by technology giants such as Apple, Google, and Facebook, including tools, platforms, and services.

Virtual reality accounts for about 60% of the total turnover, but by 2023 things should be reversed: AR will travel at a development rate of 73.8%, higher than virtual reality. The demand for sectors such as tourism and retail should be driving AR. According to analyses by Statista, IDC, and Goldman Sachs, by 2020, more than 1 billion users will use AR applications and services, helping to fuel a market that is estimated to exceed $215 billion within two / three years.

A parallel statement can be created for the hardware-software division: at the moment, about 65% of the sector's turnover is the prerogative of hardware devices, such as virtual reality viewers. But the demand for software solutions is set to travel faster, approaching these percentages. The USA, which represents the dominant country of this new market, is destined to maintain this leadership position in the following four years, even if Canada, Central Eastern Europe, and Western Europe will experience higher rates of development.

Despite analysts making market growth estimates by unifying virtual reality and augmented reality, developers believe that augmented reality will drive the growth trends of the next few years: "where virtual reality reproduces the real world to create spaces digitally, augmented reality understands and includes the real world; AR superimposes virtual images on real environments, spaces, and images, creating a potential for customer experiences that are very different from those possible with VR," Digital Trends reports.

VR environments, by their nature, require the utmost attention from the user (who is immersed in a reconstructed environment within which he can move and interact only "digitally"), which makes the technology inadequate for real social interaction outside of a digital world.

Instead, AR makes it possible (and this is precisely where its strength lies) because it has the potential to act as an on-demand "co-pilot" in everyday life, integrating perfectly into the daily interactions that users have in the real world.

Interactions that can range from gaming to entertainment, from sports to the shopping experience, up to coming into play in business and work contexts: 64% of American consumers in the United States, even believe that augmented reality will bring benefits to the workplace, for example by facilitating collaboration between teams located in different locations or by accelerating design and innovation processes.

Companies are also in favor of these situations. That is confirmed by research recently carried out by Capgemini entitled "Augmented and Virtual Reality in Operations: A guide for investment," conducted on about 700 executives in the automotive, manufacturing, and utility sectors.

82% of companies currently implementing these solutions believe the benefits exceed their expectations. In comparison, a good 46% of respondents expect AR and VR to become mainstream within the next three years, while a further 38% expect this transition within the next three to five years.

In general, augmented reality is considered more applicable in the company by supporting a more splendid series of innovative uses precisely because of its ability to interact with reality. Some virtual reality solutions are considered capable of positively impacting businesses.

45% of companies use AR, while the percentage drops to 36% for companies that have implemented virtual reality (the rest are still in the experimental phase).

The extent of the investments and the areas of application of augmented reality

When Augmented Reality Began: Origins And Evolutionary Scenarios

The first condition of augmented reality dates back to 1968 when Ivan Sutherland developed the first AR glasses. Also, in the same year, the origin of the first VR viewer can be traced back when Ivan Sutherland, together with Bob Sproull, developed a primitive solution with wireframe graphics similar in design to the cumbersome mechanical machinery called Sensorama of 1962, the earliest known example of immersive multisensory technology by Morton Helig.

In the 90s, virtual time reality was coined by Jaron Lanier so that an organized vision of how portable devices, the Internet, and GPS can come together to give life to devices capable of increasing or enriching the level of information in the real world.

Even if the first projects were not very successful, in those years, the foundations were laid that allowed:

in 2015 to see tools such as Samsung Gear VR, Google Cardboard, and Oculus Rift on the market, technologies that will enable us to be catapulted into another world, into another room, into an environment different from the one in which we are physical;

in 2016 to witness the mass diffusion of AR, mainly thanks to the Pokémon Go game, which allowed us to understand the novelty and the difference with VR: bringing digital content simply and immediately into the physical world.

However, the phenomenon has exploded in recent years and has turned the spotlight on the new big trend, Mixed Reality (MR). Defined by analysts as the combination of virtual reality and augmented reality aimed at producing new settings and visualizations where digital and physical objects coexist and interact in real-time, Mixed Reality has a market that:

will arrive in 2024 to generate a turnover that will touch 6.86 billion dollars (according to analysts of Grand View Research).

Much more technologically advanced than VR (because it combines the use of different technologies, sensors, wearable devices, very advanced optics, and ever-greater computing power for data analysis), Mixed Reality allows you to raise AR to a superior experience enabling people to experience increasingly vast, realistic scenarios within spaces and times that become unlimited.

Giants such as Facebook, Samsung, Sony, and Nintendo are not the only ones to invest in AR-VR technologies, given that even the panorama of startups dedicated to this area is gradually expanding.

A lot is being supported in AR and VR. The application frontiers are comprehensive. Soon, there will be business opportunities in many areas, from the world of gaming to events, from health to insurance through Retail, Education, Sport, and Live Entertainment.

Augmented Reality In Marketing

Augmented reality is, in fact, a form of visual content management 2.0 that allows companies and organizations to engage customers through innovative ways: in fact, it adds new levels of information in real-time and with a high rate of interaction using mobile devices of any type, including wearable technologies.

Not surprisingly, the first experiments were in entertainment, exploiting that effect capable of capturing attention through surprise and virtual magic, making the experience with the brand as immersive and engaging as possible.

Exclusivity, personalization, and uniqueness are advantages of integrating augmented and virtual reality into the broader customer experience strategies to allow consumers to interact with the brand in a new way. People love to feel special in the eyes of brands and appreciate exclusive services; whether it's an app that allows them to try out new furniture in the apartment they live in, or that offers tips for the perfect makeup based on their skin type, the important thing is that they are personalized.

4.Stocks In The Metaverse That You Should Consider Buying

The metaverse, described as immersive and interactive virtual online environments, has piqued the interest of the investing and business worlds in recent months. As a result, companies of all kinds are pouring billions of dollars into attempting to capitalize on the internet's next big thing. This comprises Facebook, Oculus, Instagram, and WhatsApp's parent company, Meta Platforms (NASDAQ: FB). The IT behemoth intends to spend more than $10 billion each year on metaverse investments.

However, Meta isn't the only firm working on the metaverse. To ride this long-term trend, here are three metaverse stocks to invest in right now.

1. Match Group

The online dating business is dominated by Match Group (NASDAQ: MTCH). It owns several applications and services; the most well-known of which is Tinder, the most widely used mobile dating app globally. Subscription or a la carte sales currently account for most of the company's revenue. They give users access to more services and put their dating profiles in front of more potential matches. In the most recent quarter, Match Group's paying users climbed 16 percent year over year to 16.3 million, suggesting that 16.3 million people spent money on the company's various services.

This technique has proven successful so far, and it should continue to do so in the coming years. On the other hand, Match Group has stated its intention to make its services even more immersive over the next decade in its most recent shareholder letter. This will begin with video capabilities, which Match Group has already included in a number of its offerings. For example, tinder has just unveiled a "explore" area where users may connect based on the same interests or activities. In addition, it intends to introduce a virtual currency on a global scale to make purchasing virtual goods and services on the platform easier.

Match Group's most ambitious project outside of Tinder is Single Town in South Korea, administered by its latest acquisition Hyperconnect. Single Town is an experimental virtual world where singles may meet up and converse/hang out in a virtual setting utilizing avatars. Although the concept is novel and unlikely to catch on, it reflects Match Group's dedication to enhancing the services it owns.

2. Take-Two Interactive

Take-Two Interactive (NASDAQ: TTWO) is a video game developer and publisher known for titles such as (GTA) Grand Theft Auto, Red Dead Redemption, and NBA 2K. GTA, its most metaverse-like franchise, is its main revenue generator. To put things in perspective, Take-most Two's recent premium GTA game was GTA V, released in 2013. It was one of the most popular games last decade, and it continues to be a major revenue generator for the corporation.

What gives that this is possible? Take-Two Interactive published GTA Online simultaneously as GTA V. GTA Online is a virtual environment set in the fictional Southern California metropolis of San Andreas. Take-Two has consistently released upgrades and expansions for the GTA Online community since its launch, and they have fueled spending on virtual goods and services. GTA Online is probably the best example of a living metaverse in operation right now, while not as immersive as virtual reality headsets (at least not yet).

GTA Online will be released as a standalone game in March 2022 to increase the number of individuals who can interact in the virtual world. GTA VI's final release, whenever that may be, will almost certainly result in even more recurring interaction in the GTA Online universe. GTA Online will undoubtedly get more immersive as the virtual world becomes more immersive in the future decade, benefiting any Take-Two Interactive owners.

3. Roblox

Another metaverse stock is Roblox (NYSE: RBLX); however, it "flips the script" compared to Match Group and Take-Two Interactive. Rather than creating its own metaverse-like experiences, Roblox provides the tools for other developers to create their virtual worlds for users. Consider it the YouTube of video games and virtual world creation.

The bulk of Roblox's users are under 18; hence the platform's experiences are mostly geared at children. However, the business believes that with time, it will be able to improve its graphics production tools to bring its games closer to those released by professional studios such as Take-Two. With 47.3 million daily active users (DAUs) after the third quarter, Roblox is already a massive online community. These customers are splurging on Robux, the platform's in-game currency that developers can utilize to offer in-game experiences or things. (Roblox profits by taking a percentage of each transaction.)

Roblox's net bookings (their sales measure) reached $637.8 million in the third quarter, generating $170.6 million in free cash flow. As previously said, the platform is now geared at children, while Roblox is working on one of the most pure-play metaverse systems in the world. As a result, Roblox might be a terrific long-term compounder for your portfolio if you believe the trend toward increasingly immersive and virtual worlds will continue in the next decades.

10 stocks we like better than Match Group

When our award-winning expert team has a stock suggestion, it pays to pay attention. After all, the Motley Fool Stock Advisor newsletter, which they've been publishing for almost a decade, has tripled the market.

They have announced their top 10 stocks for investors to buy right now... and Match Group wasn't one of them! Yes, they believe these ten stocks are even better bargains.

Virtual Real Estate Investing

Virtual real estate investing is often considered the domain of more experienced real estate investors. This isn't entirely correct, though. With the influence of the coronavirus on the US real estate market, virtual real estate investing is here to stay. You do not need to go to other states to conduct property research. In addition, purchasing an investment property is no longer restricted by location. Anyone from anywhere may make profitable investment selections thanks to real estate investment tools and real estate investor websites.

What Is Virtual Real Estate Investing?

Virtual real estate investing is conducting property research and investment property analysis utilizing real estate investment software before purchasing an investment property. It's essentially remote real estate investing instead of the traditional method of physically attending showings. It is a cost-effective option to perform out-of-state real estate investing because it eliminates the need for travel and the costs and time connected with it. Not to add, it simplifies the process of scouting for off-market properties, which often includes physically driving around neighborhoods. Long-distance real estate investing can be done from the comfort of one's own home by virtual real estate investors.

How to Get Started in Virtual Real Estate Investing

It does not have to be difficult to become a real estate investor. You can even start it as a side venture for passive income if you have the necessary real estate resources. However, because you are no longer bound to your city, virtual real estate investing gives up a lot of alternatives for any budget and investment goals. Purchasing rental property outside of your state may be more profitable for you. So, if you're ready to put this method to work for you, here's how to get started:

How to Choose a Real Estate Market

Long-distance real estate investing can be perplexing at first since there are so many options to consider. If you don't know where to begin, pick a state that interests you. It might be a state with favorable Airbnb regulations or ideal for a holiday property. It might also be a property with no rent control and a large population if you're trying to go into typical rental rentals. Then decide whether cities or towns within it could be of interest to long-term tenants or tourists. How did you figure that out? There will be visitors if there are tourist attractions, sites, or natural features nearby. To see if there will be a demand for long-term rental homes, you can look into market statistics online, such as the number of renters, the price-to-rent ratio, and the state of the job market and economy.

This stage, even with a little research, can be challenging. That is why virtual real estate investing requires real estate investment instruments. You can't know what's happening in every town's housing market, but real estate investment software like Mashvisor can. It gathers information from various listing sites to almost automate your real estate market research. Mashvisor's real estate heatmap allows you to explore neighborhoods in any city in the United States. Different types of neighborhood data can be used to do analysis:

- Traditional and Airbnb rental income
- Listing price
- Airbnb occupancy rate
- The average rate of return on a rental property (in the form of traditional and Airbnb cash on cash return)

In this manner, you can quickly learn about the housing market in the area of your choice and determine whether it is a good place to invest in real estate. In addition, it gives you a graphic representation of the real estate market study. The heatmap allows you to search for items based on essential parameters, such as cash on cash return. The map is filtered, and the corresponding neighborhoods are highlighted in green with high values. You don't need to have ever visited the location to use this data – virtual real estate investing means you know more about the investment potential than the locals.

Making a Business Decision

Buying a rental property out of state and investing close to home have one thing in common: you must conduct an investment property study before selecting a property for sale in either scenario. This entails delving deeper into a property's financials and determining if it would be a lucrative investment. Mashvisor can assist traditional and virtual real estate investors with this. The platform does this analysis is done for you by the platform, which allows you to compare alternative options. Here's a quick rundown of what the automatic analysis includes:

Expenses and possible funding sources To calculate expenditures and return on investment, enter your mortgage or cash data into the investment property calculator. Utilities, insurance, property management fees, and HOA fees are all estimated based on historic property data for the locality. As a result, you can immediately see if a certain investment property for sale is a good fit for your real estate investing plan.

This is a rental scheme. Rental income, cash flow, cap rate, cash on cash return, monthly expenses, and occupancy rate are all reported by Mashvisor. In addition, you'll get a handy side-by-side comparison of Airbnb vs. traditional renting to help you decide which rental plan is the most profitable.

The Investment Property Calculator on Mashvisor

Investigate the competition. Mashvisor lists similar rental homes in the neighborhood to make out-of-state real estate investing even easier. In addition, both standard and Airbnb rental comps are available. Size, occupancy rate, and, for Airbnbs, the Airbnb nightly rate, as well as Airbnb ratings and reviews, are all available. As a result, you'll be able to set a reasonable rental charge.

Mashvisor's Rental Comps

You can finish the sale remotely with some assistance once you've discovered your ideal investment property. In most regions, you may engage a home inspection service to visit the property without you and give you peace of mind. Then, to work on the discussions and the offer, it would be beneficial to contact a local agency. This can be done quickly over the phone or via email (listings on Mashvisor give all agents' contact details). Finally, a digital signature is required. Many documents must be signed before the transaction can be completed, not to mention leases once you have taken ownership. Most counties now accept digitally signed documents, which will save you a lot of paperwork. After all, virtual real estate investing is technologically advanced and shouldn't have a lot of paperwork.

Metaverse Virtual Real Estate Is Booming.

The Sandbox, one such virtual world, is now topping the pack in terms of traders and sales. Last week, the Sandbox had the biggest trading volume, with more than $86 million traded for land plot NFTs, while Decentraland came in second with more than $15 million traded for land plot NFTs.

What, then, is the growing appeal of purchasing a virtual parcel of land?

NFTs and play-to-earn games, such as Axie Infinity by Vietnamese studio Sky Mavis, have introduced an entire generation of individuals into shared online communities, according to Hayden Hughes, CEO of crypto social trading platform Alpha Impact. Hughes stated that when these communities grow, members have a creative drive to express themselves by owning assets in the metaverse, such as land.

"Creatives who sincerely want to express themselves, as well as speculators looking to profit, are driving the rush to acquire land in the metaverse. Unlike the 2017 ICO [initial coin offering] bubble, the metaverse has widespread adoption and a vibrant (though early) ecosystem. "Facebook / Meta isn't the market leader in this field, and the rebrand has drawn attention to the ecosystem," Hughes explained.

Not only is the demand for metaverse experiences growing, but so is the price of metaverse land, according to DappRadar. Last week, metaverse land plot NFTs in various virtual worlds accounted for five of the ten most expensive NFT transactions.

According to the data, the top grosser was the Fashion Street Estate in Decentraland, which changed hands for 618.000 MANA, or $2.42 million. However, an Axie Genesis plot – the most valuable territory in yet another stand-alone metaverse game – sold for 550 Ethereum last month (ETH). According to a tweet from the creators, this purchase was "the greatest sale ever for a single piece of digital property," with 550 ETH worth $2.48 million as of Dec. 3.

Axie Infinity, Denctraland, and Metaverse Gaming are just a few of the games available.

"Lunacia, the Axie motherland, is divided into tokenized parcels of land that operate as residences and bases of action for its Axies," according to the Axie Infinity whitepaper. Plots can be improved over time with a range of resources and crafting ingredients gathered throughout the game."

According to the developer whitepaper, Lunacia comprises 90,601 plots of land that are represented as NFTs and can be freely sold by users. However, the Genesis property in question is highly valuable due to its scarcity: the game's 90,601 plots contain only 220 Genesis plots.

This expansion of the "creative economy," also known as "play-to-earn," allows users to own their digital assets as NFTs, exchange them with others in the game, and occasionally transport them to other digital experiences, according to recent research from Grayscale Investments. As a result, projects like Decentraland are constructing an open-world metaverse in which users can log in to play games and earn MANA (Decentraland's native currency), which can be used to buy NFTs like as LAND or collectibles), vote on economic governance, or build NFTs. In addition, this architecture provides users with significant interoperability between systems as a value proposition for their time spent in-game.

Land in the metaverse, according to Matt Maximo, research analyst at Grayscale Investments and co-author of the report, is a fascinating concept because traditional real estate is valued largely based on proximity to shops, services, and other people – you're limited by the time it takes to travel from your home.

Players in several metaverses, such as Decentraland, can teleport worldwide, making travel quick and unrelated to valuation. Given the developing nature of the market, many of the higher-priced sales have come from LAND lots in desirable locations, such as proximity to prominent metaverse attractions.

"Investing in LAND is exciting, but it carries the same risks as any other emerging market." LAND and MANA owners are motivated to keep the Decentraland map small and maintain the number of parcels low, but "there will come a time where enlarging the map and producing more LAND to sell will benefit them more than the dilution of their property," he explained.

He went on to say that because LAND plots are non-fungible tokens, liquidity is considerably lower than with the underlying tokens like MANA.

"If you're in a hurry to sell, you can be compelled to sell below market value to the highest bidder, whereas if I have MANA, I can go to an exchange like Uniswap or Coinbase and make the sale instantaneously," he added.

In the Metaverse, Is There an Infinite Land?

While the metaverse's rising options have greatly incentivized property purchase as a way for players to stake their claim in a virtual environment, one potential difficulty is that land may be in limitless supply.

"As a result, it's difficult to predict how much land will be worth in the future, and buying today could be considered a dangerous investment." If digital land, for example, becomes oversupplied, supply-demand economics kicks in, and the price drops. However, for investors who wish to be among the first to own land in the digital world, the sheer amount of possibilities that the metaverse may be able to offer may outweigh the danger." BLOCKv & SmartMedia Technologies co-founder Reeve Collins told GOBankingRates.

According to Eduardo Erlo, marketing manager of blockchain-based encrypted messenger Status, the frenzy of buying digital real estate could lead to a temporary slump. Erlo went on to say that because land in the metaverse is eternally abundant, paying a lot of money for it now might be a waste of money.

He said that one way to get around the endless abundance of digital land would be for some metaverses to have built-in scarcity regarding plots of land — such as the Genesis virtual land discussed earlier — similar to the built-in monetary investment scarcity offered by Bitcoin. "It's still too early to know anything about all of this," he said, "but it's interesting to watch."

According to Grayscale, the commercial opportunity for bringing any number of metaverses to life might be worth more than $1 trillion in yearly income. In addition, revenue from virtual game worlds might climb to $400 billion in 2025, up from $180 billion in 2020.

Purchases of virtual land in the metaverse, according to several experts, can be considered an investment. According to Robert Powers, director of decentralized media at Vivid Labs, the metaverse — and the many metaverses within it — will deliver on promises and change into a dynamic virtual environment in which we will all be contributing in some manner.

However, Powers told GOBankingRates that we are still in the early days of the emerging metaverse — or metaverses because there will likely be many, not just one — and that we should be wary of speculation that leads to the kind of rapid price increases that we are seeing right now in the digital land market.

"However, this burst of innovation gives immense promise for what's to come in a more completely immersive digital environment." "Perhaps these early digital land buyers are the digital equivalents of owning the Empire State Building or New York City itself," he speculated.

Another point about the value of digital real estate is made by Dan Patterson, general partner at Sfermion, an NFT-focused investment business.

5. Payment in the Metaverse

Role of Payment in the Metaverse

Payment is described as support for online payment systems, platforms, and activities. It is the legal cash and digital currency exchange, currency trading, financial services like Bitcoin and Ethereum, and other blockchain technology. Metaverse payment will be made possible by the existence of both legal and digital currencies. Based on China's present regulatory rules for digital currencies such as Bitcoin, the conflict between centralized and decentralized money will remain in the Metaverse.

Payment comprises the recognition of persons and brands, the evaluation of products or services, and the agreement on transaction details to grasp the most fundamental logic of payment.

Recognition of Individuals and Corporations

Payment is made with cards and mobile phones in the physical world, while authentication is done with passwords, biometric data, and other techniques. People keep their unique serial numbers on a secure carrier. We must investigate what constitutes a secure carrier in the metaverse. Integrating SE security chips to every metaverse device, like virtual reality headsets with SE security chips, turns it into a carrier carrying payments under the existing security route. However, the metaverse's unique identifying code for users and businesses has many possibilities, like the latest fire non-fungible token technology.

The Process of Determining Goods or Services

In the Metaverse, goods and services become digital, such as in games. If a product can alter information with easy copy, paste, and delete, and its worth fluctuates dramatically in a short period, the transaction has major flaws. This problem can be better solved using blockchain technology and NFT technologies.

Consensus on Transaction Records

According to the conventional online payment concept, the account owner will rule the world, and the likelihood still applies to the Metaverse. If there is identity verification, the accounting system will have a functioning space. It has to function similarly to the present e-commerce system's role or method so that both entities are comfortable with the transaction's substance, which the blockchain network's consensus system can do.

Preparation for Payment Companies

Meta announced the crypto initiative in Libra in 2019. The giants were already studying the payment systems required by the Metaverse before the metaverse buzz. Libra hopes to be a new decentralized blockchain network, low-volatility crypto, and smart contract system to provide a new avenue for credible financial service innovation. Libra is the keeper of a "basket of currencies" made up of international legal currencies, sometimes known as "stable currencies."

Participating institutions started to withdraw because of the multi-national compliance challenges. Therefore, Libra was rebranded Diem and focused on the US dollar stable currency. Furthermore, Meta is actively marketing the digital currency wallet concept, and its Novi division just conducted a small-scale experiment.

After being rebranded as Meta, it can securely manage payment channels and establish a solid basis for its metaverse plan's growth with the support of its crypto project structure. Domestic enterprises have not developed preparations for Bitcoin projects in advance due to governmental constraints, but there have been efforts to support virtual reality scenarios.

Alipay debuted VR Pay in 2016. The user places an order by selecting the product on the smartphone VR platform or VR App, confirming the purchase, entering the payment link, selecting Alipay, and clicking to complete the payment.

Finance and Payment in the Metaverse

In principle, Alipay's VR Pay continues the scheme based on Alipay's account framework. It is still a digital payment that falls within the e-commerce payment class. Furthermore, several banks use VR technology to enhance the customer experience.

Many banks, like Industrial and Commercial Bank of China, Bank of China, and Hua Xia Bank, presented virtual reality equipment during the 2016 China International Finance Exhibition to give consumers a fresh financial service experience. The Guangdong branch of China Construction Bank finished the design of the "Golden Bee" maker space in 2016. Through a 6-and-a-half-minute virtual reality experience video, the Guangdong Branch of China Construction Bank and Heixia.com partnered to develop the VR experience. The potential use case of virtual reality systems in customer experience, financial transactions, scene presentation, and other areas was discussed. Guangzhou Rural Commercial Bank put up a virtual reality business hall at the 6**th** China (Guangzhou) International Financial Exchange Expo, where clients may explore information and do self-service purchasing.

Nevertheless, at the time, banks' understanding of virtual reality was still limited, and most employed virtual reality technology to deliver information. Therefore, it fell short of the current Metaverse interoperability. Exploring how to locate situations and give services in the Metaverse will become a popular issue for financial institutions in the nearest future.

Unsolved Problems

Payments in the Metaverse may get more difficult in the future. For instance, consider the present game sector. The pricing of the same game varies according to the console platform, as does the division situation. Accounting needs vary depending on the platform sharing method, copyright, suppliers, and so forth.

There will be exchange rate issues if Metaverse has cross-border transactions paid in regular legal tender. SWIFT has introduced many initiatives to increase the ease of cross-border transactions, including GPI and SWIFT Go. Furthermore, the Group of Twenty (G20) has struck a deal and introduced the "G20 Roadmap on Strengthening Cross-Border Payments," which includes development ideas to enhance the ease of global cross-border transactions clearly and concisely to benefit Metaverse's development.

Furthermore, Chinese authorities are presently focusing on ethics' largely unnoticed issue. The financial and payment demands in the virtual world will eventually expand as the Metaverse grows in popularity. The Metaverse exists in parallel to the physical world, yet it is linked to it, and there are numerous options. This is the issue.

For example, suppose a woman uses a smart sex gadget. In that case, a hacker accesses the device, gains authorization to use the sex device, and issues a command to harm the woman severely. Will this be investigated as a case of rape? Another example is a user who acquires device rights remotely by paying a charge and instructing whether he is accused of prostitution with a woman's agreement.

Furthermore, there may be inconsistencies between digital currency and the Metaverse's physical financial system. The digital currency in the game can be used to purchase a variety of digital products in the game environment. Once a game's impact has grown sufficiently, its game props and currency will be rooted in value with physical currency, like a rare tool or a skin valued at thousands of Renminbi. The digital currency in the game and the physical currency have an exchange rate.

The Metaverse is no different. Virtual products have a specific worth if a virtual environment has enough impact and consumes enough user time. The most straightforward example is that Q coins will be able to buy buns in the future, and game coins will refuel. There is a financial oversight issue. However, a decentralized virtual currency with virtual props and impossible to monitor supervision will significantly influence the present financial system.

Need for Blockchain Payment System

Matthew Ball's Metaverse framework addressed the payment difficulty as the most difficult so far. According to him, the payment choices are so inefficient, unjust, and authoritarian. So, we may never have a Metaverse we expected until we transition to a blockchain-based system, which has its own set of issues.

Transaction fees and time delays are inherent in the current traditional payment systems. Virtual environment-based payment systems are considerably more expensive and inefficient built on these payment mechanisms. Similarly, distribution networks (consoles, Apple, etc.) lock in customers and developers by imposing hefty fees on the latter and excluding payment rivals.

Because mobile is so prevalent and vital for mass-market development, existing metaverse platforms end up paying Apple and Google Play the majority of their revenue. However, their drawbacks are mostly decentralized, which renders them inefficient and costly energy. For example, although Roblox's income-sharing agreement is tough for its creators, Apple takes a large blow itself. Blockchain and non-fungible tokens offer a potential fix and alternative to all of this.

Because of these flaws, practically all non-fungible token platforms save as much data as they could on centralized databases instead of the blockchain network. Non-fungible tokens rely on vulnerable "pointers" that might go offline at any time. Given this, it is unsurprising that some people consider the blockchain a major drawback. Do not forget that the virtual economy currently produces over $50 billion yearly and encompasses hundreds of billions of hours of use—all without using cryptocurrency or blockchain technology.

Blockchain-based payment methods for the Metaverse have some promise. However, most current ones place the blockchain cart ahead of the digital world horse.

The recent $150,000 purchase of a CryptoPunk NFT by Visa might be the first evidence that these limited-edition digital assets are being treated seriously for commerce. Until recently, the selling of these "non-fungible" assets has been connected with a high-priced piece of art, but Visa's acquisition, although also about art, is mostly about demonstrating Visa's competence in the field of employing non-fungible tokens for commerce to firms. Indeed, Visa has a future goal, according to a study released in conjunction with the CryptoPunk purchase.

Alethea AI that claims to have invented the world's pioneer "intelligent NFT," recently secured US$16 million in investment to construct a metaverse occupied with its avatars, and it is along similar lines in terms of the larger metaverse's potential, paired with the crucial function of NFTs. The talking, intelligent NFTs (iNFTs) produced by Alethea, which can conduct human-like dialogues, will populate the Metaverse.

Supporters of a completely decentralized Metaverse, in which non-fungible tokens play a key role in supporting the DeFi required for this meta-project to exist, convened recently in Paris for the Ethereum event EthCC. The importance of permissionless, trustless financial services with a high transaction rate for a Metaverse to function effectively was discussed by key speaker Ben Lakoff, co-founder of NFT-protocol Charged Particles. The Metaverse would also demand the storage and inalterability of a significant quantity of data, where blockchain technology comes into play.

Aside from the technological limitations of a space capable of supporting thousands, if not millions, of individuals online in the same virtual environment at the same time, one thing is certain: A DeFi financial design involving non-fungible tokens, which you might call the "MetaverseFi," is likely to be critical to its success.

Clearly, any major actors in the Metaverse, such as Meta and Epic Games, will have to comply with the upcoming DeFi cryptocurrency laws when developing decentralized payment systems in the metaverse.

Outlier Venture, a UK blockchain VC firm, discovered that a cryptocurrency-decentralized core is essential for a metaverse's success:

> "It requires its own economy and native currencies, where value can be earned, spent, lent, borrowed, or invested interchangeably in both a physical and virtual world, and most importantly without the intervention of a governing system."

Although the Metaverse may be virtual, I think its usage of non-fungible tokens and decentralized finance to bring it to life is solidly grounded in reality.

6. How Will NFTs Affect The Metaverse?

NFTs can potentially upend the conventional social network paradigm of user contact, socialising, and transaction in the metaverse by upsetting the existing social network paradigm. Learn how non-fibre technologies (NFTs) might cause havoc in the digital world.

An Open And Fair Economy

At the moment, people and companies may transfer their real-world assets and services to a virtual decentralized environment called the metaverse, a virtual decentralized environment. One method of bringing more real-world assets into the metaverse is using novel gaming models in conjunction with interoperable blockchain games.

Play-to-earn gaming models are one such way that engages players in blockchain games and allows them to do more with their time. NFTs enable users to participate in financial in-game economies in the metaverse and get incentives in exchange for the value that they provide, allowing them to make money while they play. In the metaverse, play-to-earn games are also fair since participants retain complete ownership of their assets rather than having their assets owned by a single game entity, as is the case with most conventional games.

When it comes to taking part in these virtual financial in-game economies, Binance NFT's IGO launches provide a range of in-game assets from gaming projects that players may gather and integrate into a variety of virtual financial in-game economies for usage. Such in-game NFTs are in great demand, as seen by the reaction to IGO debuts, when all NFTs were sold out within minutes of the game's official launch. Axie Infinite (AXS), My Neighbor Alice (Alice), and many other popular play-to-earn games are instances of this kind of game.

On addition, gaming guilds that specialise in play-to-earn gaming will be important in increasing the overall appeal of this kind of gaming. As facilitating middlemen, guilds purchase in-game NFT resources like as land and assets, then lend them out to players who wish to utilise them in their separate virtual worlds to earn returns on their investments. Guilds that encourage players to play for money then take a tiny percentage of the money earned.

This helps foster an open and fair economy by allowing players who do not have the necessary funds to begin playing via guilds, which gives them an advantage. Players of all skill levels may benefit from guilds because they reduce the entrance barrier to play-to-earn games and make it more equitable for everyone to have a chance to participate in the metaverse economy. Briefly stated, guilds assist to jumpstart virtual economies in the metaverse by making NFT resources more available to all players.

YGG (Yield Guild Games) is an example of this, as they construct a worldwide community of metaverse players that contribute to the virtual worlds to receive in-world benefits, generating cash via the rental or sale of YGG-owned assets for a profit.

Because users may trade their NFT assets, such as in-game assets and digital real estate, on NFT markets such as Binance NFT, in-world assets can demand real-world value as well as virtual currency value. Because of their use in certain modules of the metaverse, the economic worth of NFTs delivered in-game may be determined. This provides users with the flexibility to pick the sort of material they wish to develop, such as popular assets that appeal to a wide range of consumers, original digital artwork, or specialised NFTs that confer certain skills and appearances in games to players.

Metaverses create an open and fair economy that is supported by the intrinsic qualities of the blockchain, such as immutability and transparency. Furthermore, prices are determined by the basic rule of supply and demand, based on the scarcity and on-chain value of an NFT according to its application, preventing the potential of pumping and fake value inflation.

The gaming drops offered by Binance NFT are an example of the facilitated style of operation available in the metaverse economy.

The weekly IGO releases include fundamental in-game materials from gaming projects, allowing players to get a head start early in the game in the NFT gaming sector. Aside from that, Mystery Boxes drops are only available in play-to-earn games and contain a variety of valuable items.

In addition, users may find and trade NFT products obtained in-game on the Binance NFT secondary marketplace. To assist NFT newcomers in getting started on the marketplace, Binance NFT curates a daily list of suggestions for NFT collections and creators that can be seen on the homepage, as well as rating boards that highlight the most popular NFT sales, collections, and creators.

An Extension of Identity, Community And Social Experiences

In metaverses, NFTs will also play an important part in the formation of identity, the formation of communities, and the formation of social experiences. The possession of specific NFT assets might indicate a user's support for a project or express viewpoints on the virtual and real worlds to other users. This enables like-minded people who have such NFTs to form groups to exchange experiences and generate material. The NFT avatars that are now trendy are an example of such NFTs.

A player's actual or imagined self is represented by their NFT avatar. In the metaverse, players may use their NFT avatars as access tokens, allowing them to enter and bounce between various regions. As a result, NFT avatars serve as an extension of our real-life identities, allowing us to curate and construct our virtual identities in the metaverse while maintaining complete ownership and control over our virtual identities.

Owning avatar NFTs entitles you to virtual membership in a plethora of unique experiences in both the metaverse and the actual world, hence improving your sense of belonging and social interaction. Already, NFT avatars are assisting in shaping the experiences and surroundings of the metaverses via content production and the development of new businesses and organisations.

The Bored Ape Yacht Club and CryptoPunks collections, for example, are vibrant instances of identity-shaping avatars that provide their proprietors special privileges and access to gated communities of rich people with protected material and even offline private events. Exclusive events with entry fees linked with NFTs draw attention to NFTs' function as value carriers that bridge the gap between the digital and physical worlds.

To find and acquire NFT avatars, you may go to the Binance NFT Marketplace, which offers a wide range of inexpensive NFT avatar options to choose from.

Property Ownership: Virtual Real Estate

Through the usage of NFTs, people may claim complete ownership of their virtual lands and spaces in the virtual world. The blockchain technology that underpins the asset allows users to show ownership of the asset and build their virtual real estate as they see fit.

Some of the applications for virtual real estate in the metaverse include the sale of land for profit, the rental of land for passive income, the construction of different buildings such as online stores on existing property, and the hosting of social gatherings.

For instance, Decentraland, in conjunction with Adidas, recently organised a virtual fashion show where designs were auctioned off as non-fungible tokens (NFTs), serving as an example of the metaverse's digital real estate sector. Musicians are also taking an interest in virtual real estate, since it allows them to perform and sell National Football League tickets and products online.

The Metaverse's Long-Term Prospects

Even though they are still in the early phases of development, metaverses have the potential to provide a plethora of new social and financial possibilities via the usage of NFTs and new methods for people to communicate with one another congregate, to earn, and to trade.

Metaverses and NFT blockchain gaming will become integral parts of Web 3.0, an era in which real-world businesses expand into the digital space and users discover the versatility of such environments, thanks to the incorporation of virtual reality, video games, social media, and cryptographic elements.

NFT ownership, we feel, is essential in the coming metaverses and will open the door to a plethora of new possibilities. According to the company, interested users may utilise the Binance NFT Marketplace to find, gather, and trade unique NFT assets while also traversing the metaverse.

Some of the most important things to understand about the Metaverse

Facebook recently rebranded as Meta, reflecting the company's increased emphasis on the "metaverse," and Microsoft has now revealed that it will also enter this market shortly.

In his proposal, Meta suggests that the metaverse will ultimately enable us to participate across educational, work, and social situations, while Microsoft seems to be concentrating its efforts for the time being on the virtual office environment.

However, the question remains as to what the metaverse is and to what degree we should put our faith in the image being offered to us as being important to our everyday lives.

The concept itself is not a new one. In his 1992 cyberpunk book Snow Crash, science fiction author Neal Stephenson invented the word "metaverse," describing a 3D virtual environment in which individuals, represented by avatars, might interact with one another and artificially intelligent entities.

Many individuals have attempted to impose their meanings on the metaverse, as they would with any grand vision of a future that has not materialised. If you are unfamiliar with the concept, it may be beneficial to grasp some of the characteristics expected from a metaverse.

1. A virtual world:

I believe that this is the most significant aspect of a metaverse. Exploring it using a computer, game console, smartphone, wearable technology, or other device, and taking in the 3D images and music along the way, would be a rewarding experience. Essentially, the notion is that by doing so, you will feel more present in the metaverse, and hence less present in the real world (where your body stubbornly remains).

2. Virtual reality.

This will need the use of a virtual reality headset. The idea behind this is that you get immersed in the virtual environment, which allows you to feel even more present – at least until you come across anything that is still part of your daily life, such as a coffee table.

3. Other individuals.

The metaverse is a social environment. There are a plethora of other individuals there, all of whom are represented by avatars. According to the report, some of these avatars might be bots, virtual agents, or other representations of artificial intelligence. You may hang around with the other folks or even do stuff together if you want to be social. Given Facebook's background as a social networking site, it seems probable that the social component will play an important role in the metaverse.

Because, for example, you may utilise gaze to indicate who you are addressing, supporters of the metaverse and some experts think communication may be more natural in the metaverse than it is with video conferencing (your avatar can turn its head to look at another person). Your avatar might potentially stroll up to someone else's avatar and sit next to them to initiate a discussion.

4. Persistence.

In other words, the virtual world is always there anytime you choose to visit it. It is possible to alter it by adding new virtual buildings or other things, and the modifications are permanent the next time you come. Taking up residence and becoming a part-owner may be an option for you. In the same way that social media relies on user-generated material today – your digital creations and personal tales — the metaverse will depend on your user-generated content.

5. Connection to the real world.

It is possible that, in certain metaverse visions, virtual objects in the virtual world are representations of real objects in the real world. Using a virtual drone in the metaverse to control an actual drone in the real world is an example of this. "Digital twins" are terms used to describe the relationship between the actual and the virtual worlds.

What can I accomplish in a metaverse, and how fast can I do it?

Different organisations will most likely have their visions or even local copies of the metaverse, but they will all be linked in the same way that the internet is, allowing you to travel freely from one to the next.

It's conceivable that certain items will be more instantly attractive and useful than others, depending on their nature. Playing games would seem to be a logical progression, given that many players already love online gaming, and that certain games have already made their way into the metaverse to some extent.

Additionally, the thought of being able to socialise or meet with people while feeling as if you're really in the same room with them in person is intriguing - especially in these era of pandemics.

We don't have a good picture of what Meta's metaverse offerings will be like just yet. According to CEO Mark Zuckerberg, the announcement of the rebranding included several possible alternatives. According to some predictions, a hologram may emerge at a real meeting, or you could play chess with someone on the other side of the globe on a virtual chessboard overlaid on the actual world.

According to Facebook's vision, the metaverse will serve as our future interface to the internet. However, it remains to be seen whether we will be able to access all internet services through 3D virtual worlds and virtual reality headsets in the future.

Despite several huge firms' efforts to bring virtual reality headsets to market in recent years, including Facebook's acquisition of Oculus, they still look to be a rather specialised technology.

I believe that Facebook will need to be in this for the long haul, and that their vision of the metaverse will be several years away from being a (virtual) reality shortly.

A final observation

However, although Stephenson's initial vision of the metaverse was immensely thrilling, it also had many potential dangers, both in the online and real world, ranging from addiction to crime and the collapse of democratic institutions, among other things. It's worth noting that giant businesses controlled the vast majority of Stephenson's metaverse, with governments reduced to the status of mostly inconsequential paper-shuffling outposts.

Given the present conflicts between big companies and governments across the globe over privacy, freedom of expression, and internet hazards, we should take a close look at what sort of metaverse we want to build and who will be in charge of creating, owning, and regulating it, before moving forward with it.

7. Metaverse and Cryptocurrency

It is important to understand that the metaverse does not have to incorporate blockchain to exist, but to make the ecosystem more equitable and more secure for all participants, blockchain will play a key role in its development. With the metaverse, humans will evolve as a fully developed digital species.

Crypto meets Metaverse

Digital assets and cryptocurrencies seem to be the most vertical imperative in driving the emergence of a true metaverse. Therefore, we hear and see NFTs everywhere.

Non-fungible chips are the first step in integrating individual ownership with digital resources. A non-fungible token (NFT) is a digital item that can be created (invented), sold or purchased on an open marketplace and owned and controlled by any individual user, without the permission or support of a centralized company.

For digital items to have real and lasting value, they must exist independently of an entity that can decide to delete or disable the item at any time. What NFTs enable for the first time is a decentralized digital representation and a digital ownership layer through which deficit, uniqueness, and authenticity can be transparently managed.

Therefore, cryptography can be the necessary cornerstone for metaverses.

Why know Metaverse?

There are many cryptographic projects that are trying to develop a complete digital ecosystem based on blockchain. And because it is based on blockchain, we can participate in projects by owning their chips. One of those projects that I admire these days is Decentraland.

Decentraland is a 3D space where you can build virtual worlds, play games, explore museums full of NFT art, attend live concerts, etc. It works in a standard web browser to give you access to cryptocurrency and NFT features. You can buy and sell properties, create and sell virtual art for art galleries or build worlds. Several companies have invested in land in Decentraland and some of them may be willing to pay qualified builders for its development.

The Best Cryptocurrencies for Investing in the Metaverse

Because of what we have said, it is easy to understand how the market for cryptocurrencies related to augmented reality is rapidly expanding. Investing in Crypto Metaverse tokens could prove to be extremely productive, so let's see which are the best ones currently available on the market.

Decentraland (MANA)

The Decentraland platform with MANA tokens allows its players to purchase portions of land and use them to build/realize what they most desire (concerts, recreational spaces, land used for car driving tests). The owners of these assets are able to get real gains generated by the value imported by all users who interact with them. MANA token holders also have the right to vote on any changes that are proposed for the system, since it is based on DAO (Decentralized Autonomous Organization) technology.

Where you can buy:

https://www.etoro.com

https://www.binance.com/it

Axie Infinity (AXS)

It is a game inspired by the Pokémon universe. In fact, players can buy through AXS tokens (NFT) small animals, breed them and make them fight each other. By completing the different activities proposed by the game, users can earn, invest or sell more AXS tokens. Axie Infinity works by operating on the Ethereum blockchain, connected to Ronin (a sidechain that lowers commission costs and speeds up transactions).

Metaverse Index (MVI)

This token allows investors to invest in the world of cryptocurrencies related to the Metaverse without participating in gaming activities or virtual gaming platforms. In fact, investors can leverage the MVI token as a true ETF for the Crypto Metaverse, capturing tokens that offer various services in virtual reality environments. However, the tokens must be developed on the Ethereum blockchain and their capitalization must be greater than $50 million.

The Sandbox (SAND)

This metaverse allows its users to create, sell, and purchase unique items for use within the game experience. It is based on three main components: VoxEdit (a tool used to create the unique items or turn them into NFT SAND), the Marketplace (where artists, leveraging blockchain technology can sell their creations), Gamers (those who bring the Metaverse to life through their avatars, interacting and operating in the virtual world along with other users). SAND is an ERC-20 token based on Ethereum blockchain.

Somnium Space (CUBE)

In Somnium Space it is possible to create, buy and exchange digital worlds and NFT resources. The peculiarity of this system, based on CUBE tokens, is the fact that before making purchases or exchanges, users can experience and try the virtual worlds created. It will be possible to dine in a restaurant designed by another player, or visit an exhibition in a museum. CUBE is also based on Ethereum blockchain and is an ERC-20 utility token.

8. Metaverse, Marketing, Retail and E-commerce

Although this is a technology in the development phase, with projects that are still embryonic or that have not abstractly exploited all the possibilities offered by a metaverse, the attention to this world that combines the real with the virtual is very high among marketing and communication players as well as retail and eCommerce operators.

If the metaverse acquires the power to involve people that social networks have acquired since 2008, it is clear that we are facing the new frontier of virtual interaction, capable of revolutionizing the dynamics through which to promote a product or a service, acquire and retain customers.

In the metaverse coexist and integrate with each other: virtual shops, augmented reality, NFT, streaming services, information sites, video platforms, eCommerce portals and more.

The big digital players become the "creators" of digital worlds made of patents, software, platforms, collaborations, partnerships aimed at making people live a second life (or first life) in which they can transfer a substantial part of their daily life and preserve their identity.

Among the pioneers are large fashion companies. For example, Gucci with the virtual version of the Gucci Garden open to the public within the Roblox platform. Or again, Balenciaga with its skins for Fortnite.

Of interest for industrial development is the partnership concluded between Nvidia and BMW. The objective? The creation of a "virtual original" of a factory in order to virtually plan new workflows, before applying them to the physical factory. Here's another example of the potential of real-virtual interaction systems.

Not only. In an increasingly phy-digital market, where the shopping experience must be increasingly immersive, eCommerce and retail could see with the advent of the metaverse a further boost.

Imagine having a coffee with a friend of yours, sitting at a table in a coffee shop. You describe the t-shirt you would like to buy and in an instant a selection of t-shirts flashes in your peripheral vision. Digital images scroll by. Your virtual assistant, based on your preferences and thanks to artificial intelligence, fine-tunes your selection.

- And there's the t-shirt you wanted.
- With a simple gesture, you can buy the t-shirt and get (or purchase) an NFT version to dress up your holographic avatar.
- Say hello to your friend. You slip off your glasses.
- You've had coffee with a friend, purchased a t-shirt, all from the comfort of your couch at home.
- That's one of the potentials of the metaverse.

Merging the physical world with the virtual one, in order to significantly enrich the daily experiences of users.

The metaverse as a tool to offer greater access to consumers than today's material world. Or, the metaverse as a way to improve the eCommerce experience, responding to corporate and consumer needs. In other words, the speed of an online purchase, with the experience of an in-store purchase.

The eCommerce Metaverse: Instructions for Use

Since there is no single metaverse, it is not possible to provide unambiguous instructions.

Some rules of caution are, however, necessary.

Read the terms and conditions (if any) before creating your avatar and accessing the metaverse.

Do not provide sensitive and/or personal information, if you are not sure of the reliability of the platform or of the user-avatar you are interacting with.

Always remember that if you act as a consumer, there are more favorable rules.

Fashion 3.0 in the Metaverse

This evolution of the tech giants will also strongly influence fashion and sales.

Since 2020, everything has moved into the realm of ether and virtual; fashion houses will be doing shopping experiences through glasses and viewers: you can comfortably shop and try on clothes from the couch at home

Thanks to the visor you will find yourself in the virtual world: you will be able to follow office meetings, go shopping, try on items from the new collection of your favorite designer or play.

It will be the triumph of secure shopping and customers will find virtual objects thanks to Blockchain and NFT technology and can easily access exclusive content: works of art, sports tokens collectibles.

In addition to Facebook there are Microsoft, Roblox, Epic Games, Tencent, Alibaba and ByteDance who have invested millions of dollars on the development of the project.

Mesh for Microsoft Teams will allow us to participate in video calls in avatar version even without glasses or visors: Microsoft's cloud will realize virtual reality by exploiting artificial intelligence.

Alibaba is working to prepare for the new virtual e-commerce, while ByteDance (which controls TikTok) is figuring out how to evolve video in 3D format.

Ayayi new fashion icon

Ayayi is the Chinese digital influencer so realistic that she looks real.

Lil Miquela, a virtual pop star as well as model and influencer, had appeared in 2020.

Ayayi is a "meta-human" influencer.

Influencer marketing is the main promotion tool in China for brands that want to conquer the market and the use of KOLs (Key Opinion Leaders) is one of the most efficient strategies.

The French maison Guerlain, a brand of perfumes, cosmetics and skin care products has expressed its willingness to collaborate with Ayayi.

The Metaverse, avatars and the virtual will be the future of fashion and not only.

Big giants have already understood this, but also luxury brands such as Gucci and Louis Vuitton.

The challenge will be to move from social networks to the virtual world, creating new sales channels and dressing in digital, in pixels and not in fabric.

A bet already faced by many, for example the capsule collection of Moschino for The Sims, that of the Metaverse will be a great challenge.

9. Building The Metaverse Experience

Things are moving quickly, and if you want to stay up with your users and rivals, you will have to get started right now. Here's a fast selection of resources to help you learn more about the metaverse and how you can use the underlying technology to generate value for your brand.

3D Modelling

3D modeling is crucial to building metaverse experiences. Hence why this section is important. We have provided a detailed guide to help you refresh your 3D modeling knowledge or set you on the path of learning. Either way, there are tremendous opportunities for creators to develop experiences that will shape the future of metaverse. You want to pursue 3D modeling as a job or a pastime. We will show you how to get started.

3D modeling necessitates a unique blend of technical and creative abilities. It is a career-oriented field with a lot of promise, especially in the metaverse. 3D modeling offers a variety of applications that may be useful in the virtual world, and it is a talent worth learning.

While it is a frequent notion that the entry barrier is quite high, this is not the case. In reality, even if you do not like to put in a huge amount of money, it is not difficult to get started with 3D modeling today. You are ready to go as long as you have a computer with a good processor and some form of a graphics card.

The fundamental concept behind 3D modeling is to build three-dimensional shapes that can be viewed in various ways. The ultimate result may be a static scene generated from a certain angle or a complex model that can be viewed from any aspect.

When dealing with 3D, you normally begin with a simple geometric shape (such as a cube, sphere, or cylinder) and alter it using different modifiers until it matches what you attempt to create. Of course, that is an oversimplified version; most complicated models are made up of several smaller shapes adjusted separately.

The basic procedure is changing their shapes on several layers. You may either move the entire object around (or apply many other changes, such as resizing or rotating it). Alternatively, you can divide it into its constituent parts and deal with them individually.

When working with a cube, for instance, you can alter one of its sides. You may also deal with specific vertices or simply one edge of that side (the corner points that connect edges). Using different modifiers, you may quickly apply significant changes to such shapes.

Choice of 3D Modeling Software

3D modeling was often thought to be a discipline that needed sophisticated commercial software to enter. 3ds Max, Maya, Cinema 4D, Houdini, and other prominent software packages are still used today. Blender, the only effective free software, existed back then, but it was not the Blender that most of us are familiar with now.

In terms of functionality, UI/UX, simplicity of use, and community support, Blender may easily compete with the main leaders in the industry today. Several studios are now expressly looking for Blender expertise, which was not the case a few years ago.

With that in mind, Blender is the ideal option if you do not wish to spend a huge amount of money on commercial software. It is capable of taking you as far as other common options available on the market. Blender is expected to grow in popularity in the foreseeable future as the development of the virtual space continues.

3D Modeling Hardware Requirements

Hardware Requirements

One of the most common criticisms of 3D modeling is that it needs powerful gear to get started. That is no longer the case.

Modern 3D programs such as Blender can be operated on even a subpar PC with an incorporated graphics card. When dealing with sophisticated modifiers or when your scene becomes huge, editing may take a while, but you will not be doing any of that when you initially begin.

A faster computer immediately translates to quicker rendering speeds when it comes to rendering. This implies that if you have the time to wait for your renderings to complete, you can get away with a low-powered machine. Keep in mind that the speed differential might be fairly dramatic. A computer with a powerful graphics card, such as an RTX 3070, could render a scene in seconds, but an older system may take days.

There are internet rendering farms that could help with this, but they are not free. This is a better way than investing a few thousand dollars on a modern computer.

3D Modeling for Business

Suppose you have decided to pursue 3D modeling for business purposes, such as building a metaverse experience rather than just as a creative pastime. In that case, you will want to concentrate on a few key areas. Selling unique models is a fantastic place to start. However, it is a saturated field.

You might also consider selling your renderings to individuals and brands in other formats, such as conventional art (prints or t-shirts). To summarize, 3D modelers are in high demand in the metaverse development industry.

You should research the industry and identify the essential abilities you will need to succeed. In this sense, each area of 3D modeling is distinct, and you will have to spend some time experimenting until you find what you want to achieve.

Getting Started with 3D Modeling
Join various 3D modeling platforms if you have determined you are ready to pursue 3D modeling. One of the best things about 3D modeling is that the community is well-developed. There are usually plenty of individuals willing to assist you and address any problems you could have.

CAD Modelling

Installation
We will begin with the installation of the CAD software known as AutoCAD. AutoCAD is not a free program; it costs 185 dollars a month to subscribe. It costs $1775 per year. As a result, it is a little expensive. You do, however, have a choice. If you are a beginner, Autodesk provides a free trial. But, in my perspective, it is legal if you can buy this even for a short period.

Free trial
The free trial period will last 30 days. Free trials are available for the following options.

AutoCAD WIN/MAC

Architecture toolset WIN

Electrical toolset WIN

Map 3D toolset WIN

Mechanical toolset WIN

MEP Toolset WIN

Plant 3D toolkit WIN

Raster Design toolset WIN

AutoCAD mobile app

AutoCAD web app

AutoCAD 2020 System Requirements

- **Operating System: Microsoft Windows 10 (64-bit only), 8.1 (64-bit only), or Windows 7 SP1 (64-bit only)**
- Processor: 2.5 GHz (3+ GHz recommended)
- Memory: 8 GB (16GB recommended)
- Disk Space: 6.0 GB
- Displ1920 x 1080 resolution with True Color

Identify the User Interface

You may now launch AutoCAD after it has been properly installed. There is a user interface with a lot of buttons and text on it. Therefore, let us have a look at what you need to understand about this.

AutoCAD is mostly used for drawing. Beginners, on the other hand, may use this to begin 3D modeling. The rationale for this is that all of the fundamental commands can be learned quickly using real-life examples. Let us have a look at what is included in these interfaces.

Drafting and Annotation Interface

- Application Button

The application button can be used for a variety of file-related operations. In addition, the application button provides access to the printing and file exporting operation options.

- Toolbar for Quick Access

The quick access toolbar has features for quick save, print, open redo, and undo.

- The Ribbon Area

The ribbon area has a variety of tools. Line drawings, modification, and editing options are all found in the ribbon area when you're using the drafting interface.

- File Tabs

In this tab, you can see which files are open and which are being worked on.

- UCS

In 3D modeling, the User Coordinate System is the most significant factor. In AutoCAD, there are two major coordinates. Both the UCS (user coordinate system) and the WCS (world coordinate system) are used. Both may be altered depending on our needs and location. We may adjust the work plane and direction using them.

- Layout Tabs

The most often used layouts in AutoCAD are model and plotting layouts. These tabs allow you to switch between printing and working layouts swiftly.

- View Cube

The view cube contains all three-dimensional viewpoints. These are the views: front, back, top, left, right, and back. You may see the applicable view side of the item by simply clicking one side. You may see and view the model by clicking the edge.

- Navigation Bar

All navigation path processes are included in this. In this area, you may observe orbit, the navigation wheel, zoom function, and motion.

- Status Bar Toggle

This is a quick overview of the most often used drafting and annotation interface. This section handles all types of tracking (object tracking), workspace switching, and snap modes. You will understand more as your knowledge grows.

3D Modeling Interface

We will use this interface to learn more about 3D modeling. Only the ribbon and its choices may be changed here.

- Ribbon Tab

In the AutoCAD platform, the ribbon tab is the most often used tab for 3D modeling. This may be used for all types of solid and surface editing. The ribbon section allows you to do modeling, mesh editing, solid editing, drawings, altering, section editing, viewing, coordinates set, and layer management.

This is a quick rundown of the user interface. Let us look at how to make a simple 3D object now.

Fundamental Steps in 3D Modelling in AutoCAD

- Step 1: Decide on your units.

This is the very first thing you should do. Since you must be aware of the units on which you will be working. Millimeters, centimeters, meters, and kilometers are examples of standard units. So, you must choose which units you are going to focus on. After that, everything is modified accordingly.

- Step 2: Analyze the Model or Drawing

Before developing a 3D model, you must first examine the drawing, reference picture, or model and generalize the final product. When you examine it, you will notice that the same pieces are utilized several times and how the object's body should look from the front, rear, sides, top, and bottom, among other things.

What should the front look like, and how can it be seen from the sides? As a result, you must be familiar with the fundamentals of drawing—observations from the first and third angles. If you have done this before, you will be able to capture them in a matter of seconds.

- Step 3: Ideation

This section requires you to consider the final item. Which method should you use to get the object? The method should have the fewest steps possible, and the object should be 100% precise and rapid. Similar sections, mirrored parts, holes, tapering, bends, linkages, and other features can be seen during the examination. These types can be altered depending on the level of intricacy.

Separate modeling and putting them together can be preferable to modeling the entire item. As a result, you may extract various types of facts into your mind during the analysis phase. Everything should begin with drawing. So, stick with that for a more effective approach.

- Step 4 Modeling

Draw the picture first, then use 3D instructions to create and finish the object, according to the drawing you gave. In 3D modeling, the essential thing is to save and retain a copy.

- Step 5 Connecting Parts

In this stage, the different modeled objects are connected to form a single object. For a better tracking procedure, you may use snap tracking in this stage.

- Step 6: Finalizing

After modeling, create a "UNION" object to link all the connections and objects together. If the pieces are in distinct files, combine them before finalizing the project. If you use AutoCAD rendering, AutoCAD provides an excellent rendering solution appropriate for modeling objects.

- Step 7 Plotting

After completing all of the steps, you will need to plot, which we refer to as printing. In AutoCAD, you may print in a variety of methods. The ideal method is outlined below.

Plotting in AutoCAD in the Easiest and Fastest Way

- **Select "Visualize" tab**

- Select "Model Viewports" and then "Name"
- Make a new view name in the viewport settings and then click "OK."
- Then, on the layout switching panel, "right-click" the "+" mark.
- Then, load the “New” or “Template” layout.
- Navigate to the fully loaded layout
- Go to the "Layout" panel in the loaded layout.
- Next, go to layout viewports and choose "Named"
- Select and load the stored name.
- You may show any view by drawing on the layout.

Photogrammetry

This section will walk you through the fundamental principles of the photogrammetry workflow that is required to create experiences in the metaverse. Photogrammetry is the act of getting exact measurements from images. It entails collecting a series of overlapping images of an item, structure, people, or environment and utilizing a variety of computer programs to turn them into a 3D model.

Applications of Photogrammetry

Photogrammetry is utilized in a variety of applications. We will walk you through some of the interesting applications of photogrammetry in the metaverse.

- **Artists can document or transform a previous work of art, sculpture, or natural phenomenon into something new.**
- Designers and engineers need to reverse design or custom-fit new pieces onto an old product.
- Photogrammetry mixed with semi-automatic 3D modeling processes can help game developers save time generating items and settings—a typical metaverse application.
- Artwork and artifacts in the sphere of cultural heritage can now be conserved indefinitely and digitally restored and repaired.
- Curators at museums can create virtual collections to entice visitors.
- Photographers now have an additional dimension with which to work.
- Companies that seek to provide a 3D printing service for their most valuable things, pets, or family members can now do this with photogrammetry.

These applications demonstrate the potential of the metaverse, and the opportunities abound for developers and brands.

Now let’s delve deeper into the concept of photogrammetry and how to get started.

The Process of Photogrammetry

- Step 1: Take Images

Take a sequence of overlapping images of the thing you want to capture. For apps with low accuracy requirements, an 8-megapixel phone camera will suffice, but we suggest an 18 MP (or higher) DSLR-type camera for optimal results. The most recommended camera is a wide-angle camera as it has the least amount of lens distortion. A fish-eye lens, for instance, will not operate unless you use applications that can effectively correct it.

It is advisable to capture the images in a circle around the object. Begin with a low-angle circle, then repeat with a higher-angle circle to cover the topmost surfaces. Aim for a minimum of 50 percent overlap between every image, with 60-80 percent being optimum. Finally, take a couple more images of regions where crucial features can be found.

Take the following extra guidelines into consideration:

- **Ensure that the piece has a matte surface. Transparent items are difficult to transform. 3D scanning spray or dry shampoo spray could be used to turn reflective surfaces matte.**
- Many software programs struggle to deal with featureless surfaces. Surface scannability can be improved using shoe polish, sprayable chalk, painter's tape, and stone effect spray paint.
- The image's backdrop should have enough color contrast with the item. A chroma-key background or a newspaper, as long as it does not exhibit the same colors as the item, works well.
- Lighting must remain steady throughout the session, and a gloomy day is ideal.
- For a single object, 40-50 images are usually sufficient. The more images you take, the better, as long as you do not take them all from the same spot.
- The object must occupy a large percentage of the visual space.
- During the shot, be careful not to move the object.
- For every image, use a minimum depth-of-field (DOF) as possible and focus the camera precisely on the item.
- Use a tripod to prevent blurriness and for low-light situations that necessitate long exposure periods.

Based on the amount of the dataset, photogrammetry software programs might take hours or even days to deliver reliable results, even though they are continually improving. A machine with 16GB of RAM and an Nvidia CUDA-enabled GPU is required.

- Step 2: Upload

Open your preferred photogrammetry program and import the images straight into the project library. It is typically only a case of dragging and dropping. It is necessary to confirm the camera's compatibility for specific apps. They may cross-reference them with an internal database for the software to maximize its results depending on focal length, primary point, and image sensor format. A set of distortion variables referred to as a bundle adjustment are generated as a result of this.

The images will be examined for applicability to the photogrammetry procedure in the first phase of the software workflow. A green or red symbol, for instance, may show next to or on top of a picture in the library. If a large section of the photoset is declined and shooting a fresh batch is difficult, basic Photoshop manipulation might help. With white wall backgrounds, this is a regular occurrence. Creating a trash matte mask for every image helps to further differentiate the subject from the background. Refining the images may also help since the program will recognize similar characteristics across photos more easily if they are all of the same sharpness.

- Step 3: Using Photogrammetry Software to Create a 3D Model from Images

The photogrammetry program in the background handles the majority of the computational aspect of photogrammetry. However, additional functionalities may help enhance the results.

Image Matching
Many photogrammetry software packages convert the photoset into a 3D model completely automatically. On the other hand, some take Image Matching, sometimes referred to as Correspondence Search, as a distinct phase that the user must confirm. This enables changes to the photoset to be made before the more computationally demanding operations begin. The computer evaluates whether images are suitable for further processing and searches for overlapping regions in several images in this stage. It now saves how the photos will be stitched up, similar to how a 3D puzzle is put together.

Feature Extraction
This is, once again, a completely automated aspect of the photogrammetry operation in certain applications. It is possible to split this stage into various photogrammetry software applications for possible changes and iterations before proceeding. The program searches the images for traits that can be identified across numerous images in this stage. For this, some expert toolkits employ coded markers, a very precise solution that works on shiny, clear, and rather featureless surfaces. On the other hand, most tools employ the more generic Structure from Motion (SfM) method, which focuses on thick patterns on items like texts, wood grain, facial characteristics, and other designs. Edge points, lines, and corners are also essential elements. Some methods use an innovative system referred to as Shape-from-Shading to augment the data with lighting and shading signals.

In a process called Geometric Verification, they are internally validated to filter out false detections when all characteristics have been detected. The SfM engine provides a conversion that translates feature points between pictures to guarantee that the identified characteristics fall onto the same scene point. This is a sophisticated set of projective geometry-based algorithms.

Many photogrammetry applications, like COLMAP, enable users to observe the feature creation process in real-time. It is possible to halt the process in Meshroom if the user notices crucial locations where few characteristics have been discovered. Quality can be improved. By boosting keypoint sensitivity and matching ratio, adjusting presets, and converting the matching algorithm to A-KAZE or, in certain circumstances, a brute force technique.

Triangulation

In 1480, Leonardo Da Vinci invented a method for determining the painter's origin from an art piece. In this essential component of the SfM process, something occurs. The surface points' 3D coordinates are calculated using the scene graph generated from the previous phase. The ray cloud is created by reconstructing the lines of sight from the camera to the item. The junction of the multiple beams determines the object's ultimate 3D coordinates.

After establishing global geometry with a sparse point cloud, photogrammetry software creates a depth map by analyzing the lighting and texture of the environment. This, like a woodcarver, adds all the small touches to the 3D model to bring it to life. Advanced applications employ a technique called delighting in smoothening the illuminated and darkened portions for more homogenous lighting throughout the full surface of the model. It is even feasible to reverse-calculate ambient occlusion effects and clears them away. While a genuinely illuminated model is frequently preferred for on-screen display, a delit model is best for full-color 3D printing.

The depth map is referred to as dense reconstruction. The sparse reconstruction, which laid out all visual elements discovered previously, is then integrated into a 3D mesh format like FBX, OBJ, PLY, or STL.

The process of triangulation is carried out automatically. The user may improve the image quality by changing the Track Length, Number of Neighboring Cameras, and Maximum Points parameters. Many photogrammetry systems also let you know how many triangles are in a 3D mesh model, impacting file size and post-processing time. It is important to note that changing these variables should be done with caution because they might quickly increase processing times.

Many commercial photogrammetry software packages include extra machine learning approaches to categorize identified flora, structures, and automobiles. They can sift out moving background items like animals and people and create improved shape data based on foreground outlines, reflectivity, and brightness. Using the catenary curve fitting techniques, thin objects like steel frames and power lines may be automatically generated in 3D.

- Step 4 Post-Processing

While the analytical aspect of photogrammetry is complex, it is typically the most straightforward for the user, who simply has to drop in their photos and press a few buttons. When the 3D model has been created, the actual labor begins. Photogrammetry does not produce a waterproof mesh model that is suitable for 3D print. Floating art pieces, background sound, holes, and inconsistencies are all common issues to clear up. The item will equally need to be repositioned and resized, which photogrammetry software can perform at will.

Many software programs provide built-in post-editing capabilities; if not, a good approach is to complete the required file conversions in Meshlab and the mesh cleanup, mending, remeshing, and resculpting effort MeshMixer. This software is available for business usage at no cost.

The model will be set for 3D printing or import into a CAD system after this phase is completed and the file is stored in STL format.

LiDAR

Are you familiar with LiDAR technology? How would you feel if you could wave your magic wand and instantly know how far everything is from you? This is how LiDAR works.

After reading this, you should be on your way to becoming a LiDAR hero and start applying your skill to create the metaverse experience.

Meaning of LiDAR (Light Detection and Ranging)

LiDAR is a distance technology. LiDAR devices beam light to the ground from a plane or helicopter. The signal travels to the earth and then back to the sensor. The time it takes for the signal to return to the sensor is then measured.

LiDAR calculates a distance by tracking the time it takes for a signal to return. The word LiDAR (Light Detection and Ranging) comes from this.

How LiDAR Works

LiDAR is a technology for sampling. It puts out over 160,000 signals every second. Each 1-meter pixel receives roughly 15 signals per second. This is why LiDAR point clouds have such a large number of points.

Since LiDAR technologies are managed in a platform, they are extremely accurate. For instance, vertical precision is approximately 15 cm, and horizontal precision is only about 40 cm. LiDAR devices scan the ground from side to side while an aircraft flies through the air. While some signals may fall straight down at nadir, most will travel at an angle (off-nadir). As a result, when a LiDAR system estimates elevation, it also considers angle.

The swath width of linear LiDAR is generally 3,300 feet. New technologies such as Geiger LiDAR, on the other hand, can scan widths of 16,000 feet. In comparison to traditional LiDAR, this sort of LiDAR can cover far larger footprints.

Possibilities on LiDAR

- Elevation Models

Digital Elevation Models are topographic models of the Earth's surface. You may create a DEM using solely ground returns. However, this differs from Digital Terrain Models (DTMs), which include contours.

You may create more items by utilizing a DEM. For instance, you might create:

Slope

Aspect (slope direction)

Hillshade (shaded relief considering illumination angle)

- Digital Surface Models

LiDAR, as you have learned, looks through the trees. The light ultimately hits the earth. Then we have a return to a bare Earth. However, what about the first return to the tree?

Elevations from natural and constructed surfaces are combined in a Digital Surface Model (DSM). For instance, it adds structures, tree cover, power lines, and others.

- Canopy Height Model

The real elevation of geographical objects on the ground is determined using Canopy Height Models (CHM). This form of elevation model is also known as a Normalized Digital Surface Model (nDSM).

Take the DSM, which comprises both natural and artificial characteristics such as trees and structures. Take out these heights from the naked Earth's surface (DEM). When you remove the two, you obtain a surface of elements that reflects true ground level height.

- Light Intensity

LiDAR intensity refers to the reflective percentage. Light intensity is influenced by range, incidence angle, beam, receiver, and surface material (in particular). However, light intensity is influenced by some things. When the pulse is angled further away, for instance, the return energy diminishes.

When it comes to recognizing characteristics in land use/cover, light intensity is extremely beneficial. In light intensity photographs, impervious surfaces, for instance, stand out. This is why picture categorization, such as object-based image analysis, benefits from the light intensity.

- Point Classification

The American Society for Photogrammetry and Remote Sensing (ASPRS) gives a series of classification codes to LiDAR point categorization.

Point categorization can often fall into more than one class. Ground, forest (low, medium, and high), structure, and water are examples of these classes. Vendors frequently mark these places with supplementary classes if this is the case.

LiDAR may or may not be classified by vendors. The codes are created semi-automatically by the reflected laser pulse. This LAS categorization field is not included in all manufacturers' packages. It is normally agreed upon in advance of the contract.

Components of the LiDAR system

A LiDAR has four primary components. They collaborate to provide extremely precise and practical results:

- LiDAR sensors: Sensors on the airplane scan the earth from side to side as it moves. Typically, the signals are in the green or near-infrared wavelengths.
- GPS receivers: GPS receivers monitor the airplane's height and location. These traces are critical for obtaining correct topography and elevation data.
- Inertial measurement units (IMU): IMUs track the tilt of planes as they move. Tilt is used in LiDAR technology to determine the signal's incidence angle properly.
- Data recorders: A device records all of the signal returns while LiDAR scans the surface. These data are then converted to elevation.

10. Risks and Challenges

As it is with any new, big ideas, there are bound to be issues that arise, whether direct or indirect. In the case of the rise of the metaverse and wanting to be a part of it all, there are also some risks and challenges of which to be made aware. Some of these risks are quite similar to issues that we can already see with the Internet and social media, and others are completely new. As for challenges, developers will face many difficulties in building the technology that this innovative platform requires in order to seamlessly integrate itself into the lives of the masses, just as the Internet had done a couple decades ago.

Social Risk

Addiction

With all the advancements of the digital world, people—and, in particular, youth—find themselves drawn to technology. Therapists now deal with thousands of children who are, at various levels, so indoctrinated to their devices that, to varying degrees, they cannot live in the real world normally. With the rise of the Internet and all the good it brought with it, also came new problems, and one such is that of addiction. Whether Internet Addiction Disorder (IAD) qualifies as a true mental illness, however, remains a hot debate.

In 2016, Common Sense Media, a nonprofit organization designed to provide reviews of technology and movies for families, discovered from a survey that around 50% of teenage participants felt "addicted" to their phones, and that 75%of these people felt the urge to immediately reply to notifications (Robb, 2016). However, most of these individuals would not be using the word "addiction" in the same way as substance abuse may make a person chemically addicted by altering the brain. True addiction would be to push out everything else from that person's life, not being able to function normally socially or physically, and need an increasing amount of the substance as time progressed. This is much rarer when it comes to the Internet, which is why it is often not classified as causing "addiction."

This being said, there are children who are deeply affected by the amount of screen-time they receive. Some children arrive in therapy clinics because they truly can no longer tell the difference between what is real and what is virtual. However, even this is debated as whether or not the effects were truly caused by access to the online realm, since these children may also have other underlying issues or disorders that have passed unchecked, and this in combination with screen-time has brought to light new symptoms. Either way, the best way to understand a child who the parent feels spends too much time on technology is to consult professionals in psychology and child therapy.

So, why are online games, media, and apps so addicting? Well, this is by design; the more time users spend on a platform, the more money that platform can potentially make either from advertisements, in-app purchases, or by other methods. Video game companies often specifically create "compulsory loops" that make the player want to continue playing on and on. Expectation, leading to reward, releases dopamine in the brain and makes the user feel good, which also leads to them wanting to continue using the technology (Smith, n.d.). Examples of rewards could be completing a level of a video game or getting "likes" on a social media post as a sort of validation. The inconsistency and dependency on the user to achieve these rewards also makes the experience more exciting, thus increasing dopamine.

The metaverse plans to make technology more interactive and more lifelike than ever. It will also not only boost social media activity but will encourage people to spend even longer periods of time on its platforms than even the modern Internet. There is thus the high risk of increasing dependency on technology, especially by the youth, whose minds are still moldable and underdeveloped. This posts the social risk of new generations that will not be able to function outside of the virtual world as easily as the generations that did not have virtual and augmented reality integrated into their early lives.

The issue becomes even more nuanced in debate: Is this truly a problem with the industry, that purposely makes their technology addicting in order to keep user retention? Or rather, is this risk, instead of placing the blame on the metaverse or the Internet itself, a responsibility of parental management? After all, it is the parents who decide how much screen-time a child receives, and it is the parents who buy the devices. In this way, it can be debated that parents should be responsible for how their child interacts with technology.

Social Media

When looking out at the future of the metaverse, the social media world only seems to improve, becoming more interactive and easily accessible than ever. As mentioned, however, addiction may also become more rampant. Additionally, there is a significant challenge in successfully transferring an already large and established user database to a whole new platform. Finally, many of the problems that modern social media faces, such as concerns of privacy or safety, will not simply disappear by, say, innovating the technology that it uses or changing the name of the company.

First of all, the addiction to social media has already been touched upon; that idea of "likes" on a post releasing dopamine to the account owner. However, unlike some iPad games or browsing movies and videos, social media does have a very strong connecting aspect, bringing together people from around the world who would have never met otherwise, and allowing them to talk, exchange ideas, and learn from each other. In this case, the main issue is not something so easily overcome. The idea of FOMO, that is, **fear of missing out**, has been amplified, since people feel they **have** to keep up with all the memories of their friends, for fear of being left in the dark to something interesting. In the metaverse, where there will be so much more to see, FOMO sentiments will definitely only increase.

The challenge of transporting an established user base to another platform will be further explained in the **Developers' Challenges** part of this section, however it remains a social risk that the metaverse will inevitably undertake. In the most relevant current case, Meta is already seeing issues in its rebrand. Their main website, Facebook, still remains the face of the company, and therefore, as it stands, nobody really associates Mark Zuckerberg with the word "Meta" at all, except maybe in a mocking sense. Something similar happened in the past with another big company, Google, which, in 2015 renamed its parent company to Alphabet, Inc. in order to expand further than being a search engine. Just like with Meta, though, to the general public, the company is referred to as Google since most consumers don't care about the bureaucracy of the organization.

Finally, problems that social media presently face may be amplified with the dawn of the metaverse. Facebook was under fire when it announced its rebrand to Meta, since many critics speculated this change was in large part due to the infamy associated with the current name. Facebook had become notorious for selling the personal information of their users to large corporations in order to send them tailored, personalized ads. This was all done with the false promise that consumers would be able to have control over how their information was shared by sifting through settings. So, the world went crazy when Facebook rebranded, and it seemed like just that: changing the name so as to dissociate from bad press without actually making any underlying changes. How can one thus expect companies to act any differently—especially when it pays so handsomely—when the metaverse will just require even more personal information from users, as it truly becomes a virtual self.

This is not the only issue with social media that will be transferred to the metaverse. Internet safety has been a widespread concern since it first came online. That people can pretend to be whomever they want is a frightening thought: anyone with whom you have an online conversation could be completely different in real life to how they present themselves therein. With Facebook, measures have been taken to try and avoid this at all costs, since it undermines the very principles on which it was founded, by vetting all accounts to make sure that they are run by real people providing their real information, which is, as has just been discussed, a whole different issue in itself, but works to keep out bot-run profiles. Other metaverse platforms cannot be expected to take the exact same measures as one company, and so this begs the question: if you get attached to a life-like holographic persona in the virtual realm, and you discover that it is all falsified with malicious intent, then this would be even more damaging and harder to discover than it would be on the current Internet.

Environmental Risk

The environmental risk of the metaverse lies in blockchain mining, and one of the main concerns of developers should be to find a way to completely base the process on clean, reusable, sustainable energy if they have hopes of bringing their wide-scope dream to life.

The Developers' Challenges

Coding and Engineering

There have already been significant advancements not only in sandbox-like environments as is the case with games like Minecraft or Roblox, but also in AR and in cryptocurrency dapps—platforms like Ethereum allow direct coding straight onto the blockchain. However, this practice of blockchain coding is not so widespread or well-known as of late. That blockchain coding is quite difficult and that developers must confront their personal morality on the unsustainable qualities of their work are all risks that the metaverse must overcome in order to grow.

Growing to Be the Next Internet

In order to grow to be the next bigger and better Internet, which is the end goal of all this metaverse talk, there are many challenges along the way. The biggest one may be that of transferring established user bases to a whole new, different platform, in particular consideration of the demographic of those databases. Other difficulties include: keeping the platform decentralized, creating interoperability, and monetary issues.

Facebook remains the most popular social media platform as of 2021, however fewer youth under 18 are signing up. The demographic from 19 to around 25 years of age is the largest, and this tapers down as age increases, but it was found that many people of middle-age or older create accounts every day. Since Facebook has turned into a more adult-minded platform in general, there is some risk involved in sudden change, especially considering that VR demographics—those for whom the metaverse truly excites—are mostly young adults (Digital in the Round, 2021). These Facebook users already feel at home with the current face and it is difficult to imagine them so readily accepting a complete change in the norm.

Another difficulty that developers of the metaverse face is that age-old struggle of digital communities in keeping the system decentralized. With so many companies seeing the value and the monetary opportunity in control of the metaverse, in order to maintain balance, there must be no single power or authority of the virtual playground.

With the concept of decentralization also arises interoperability, a necessary advancement in technology that must be made in order to establish the fundamentals of a viable metaverse. Interoperability relates to a user being able to move from one app to another with the same avatar and profile. This has to be a collective effort from developers of all metaverse projects, since they all have to together find a way to let a user travel between their platforms whilst retaining their same profile.

Finally, the metaverse is **expensive**. If some virtual worlds want to be realistic in order to be more attractive to the first-time consumer, the cost of digital assets is high. This is perhaps why the involvement of such a big company as Meta is exciting for some of those pursuing the metaverse: it is a big source of funds. Still, monetary challenges also remain as a boundary for hopeful developers who would otherwise love to try their hand at coding for the platform of the future. There is so much work to get the idea of lifelike social avatars to interact in a way that is not so completely artificial as well. On platforms that already exist like **Second Life**, player avatars do not provide the same freedom of movement as a real person simply because all actions must be coded and animated. To further and further approach life-likeness, coding and animating budgets are bound to become more expensive as well.

11. What Will the Metaverse Change?

The metaverse is not only bound to change the world as we know it but the way we view it. With the implementation of 3D worlds, we will have infinite possibilities for work, travel, entertainment, and more. Let's have a look at some of the ways we will use the metaverse in the future.

Travel

The metaverse will play an important role in travel in the future. Putting on our glasses will allow us to see anywhere on earth without having to travel. The world of 3D modeling and rendering has changed drastically over the past decade. In the past, rendering and shading realistic 3D models was extremely resource-intensive, and the results were heavy graphics. Nowadays, not only do we have better 3D production methods, but our graphic cards and internet connection also process them much more quickly and efficiently.

Leading companies like Unity and NVIDIA are already developing cutting-edge 3D graphic technologies that look extremely realistic. These graphics are currently used mainly in video games, but they are gradually making their way to the movie industry. Eventually, we will have video services that will allow us to travel anywhere in the world. Better yet, we won't have to deal with crowded landmarks and may choose any weather we like.

There will be more than just real-time travel in the metaverse. One of the most exciting features of the metaverse will be time travel. Though technically we will only travel to the past we know, it is a start. Imagine traveling to the "Seven Wonders of the Ancient World" or interacting with prehistoric hunter-gatherers. The possibilities are endless.

Metaverse travel will be perfect for those who love travel but can't due to certain limitations. Professionals who work full-time and have limited time off, parents who cannot travel with young children, elderly people who have physical limitations, and people with disabilities are examples of lives the metaverse travel will change.

Entertainment

The entertainment industry is about to undergo one of the greatest changes with the upcoming metaverse. We can expect the entertainment industry to become much more interactive and accessible.

For example, the metaverse can change the way we listen to music. Artists can create music videos in the metaverse and sell tickets to their studio sessions. In addition, the size of the venue won't matter for ticket sales. The metaverse can take live concerts to the next level. We won't be restricted to a specific time or place to watch our favorite artists, and we certainly won't have to wait for our favorite bands to go on tour.

This is also true for the movie industry. Our favorite movies and television series can easily be metaverses on their own. You could ride a dragon beside Daenerys Targaryen in the Game of Thrones metaverse or enter the Matrix for the ultimate **metaverseception**. We might see a scenario like this in the latter stages of the metaverse, but interactive movie experiences are likely to be available in the initial stages. Companies like Disney and Lucas Arts already own the intellectual property rights to their universes, so they are in a good position to create a metaverse based on their franchises.

Adult entertainment is another example that is expected to benefit from the metaverse. Some experts claim that the adult industry is expected to reach $122 billion in 2026. The introduction of new internet technologies to adult entertainment is nothing new. There are many websites offering video clips and webcam interactions to their customers. The adult entertainment industry has proven to be crisis-proof, and the metaverse is sure to add its own twist to it.

Another industry that is enthusiastic about the metaverse is the gambling industry. In 2021, online gambling generated $230 billion and remained one of the most lucrative markets for online enterprises. Decentral Games, for example, offers virtual gambling using NFTs and their DG coin. We can anticipate this trend becoming more popular as the metaverse expands.

Military

The military is one of the few low-profile investors in the metaverse. Keeping up with the latest technology is a necessity for the armed forces to stay in top shape. In addition, armed forces around the world rely on simulations to train their personnel. Because the metaverse will create realistic simulations, it is only natural for the military industry to take advantage of it.

Optimus System was one of the first companies to jump on board. Their company develops and supplies military training simulators. DEIMOS, their new metaverse technology, is preparing to enter the global market. Their system creates military training environments like precision shooting, tactical behavior training, and observation training. Optimus System CEO Nam-Hyuk Kim said: “We plan to expand the development of scientific products to implement more effective, real war-like training systems based on the technologies of the fourth industrial revolution. Our company will lead the global Metaverse market with new ideas and differentiated technologies.”

Military war games and training cost organizations like NATO billions of dollars every year. With the help of metaverse technologies, not only would they be able to reduce their budget, but they could also create highly realistic training scenarios without endangering personnel.

E-commerce

Web 2.0 has made e-commerce a part of our everyday lives. Numerous business owners transitioned to digital, and countless others developed lucrative side businesses via e-commerce stores. Online deliveries have become the norm and kept the world going during the Covid-19 pandemic.

We can expect our online shopping habits to evolve with the arrival of the metaverse. The stores can create their own metaverses or come together to create virtual shopping malls. We can walk into these stores and check out the real size, color, and fit before we make the purchase.

On the other side of the metaverse, shopping will take place in the virtual reality economies themselves. Virtual land, tokens, and other goods unique to each metaverse will be available to us with cryptocurrencies. Currency for a metaverse can be Bitcoin, altcoins, or a completely original token.

Whatever the case may be, the metaverse will have a business opportunity in e-commerce. By deciding on the type of products you want to sell early on, you will have the opportunity to be among the first to enter the market. So, if you have an original idea or product, you should consider patenting it.

Workplace

Several tech giants like Microsoft have been working on creating a metaverse for the workplace. The initial plan is to create virtual conference rooms where colleagues could meet using virtual reality. During the pandemic, online meetings have already become commonplace in the workplace using apps like Zoom and Google Hangouts. Employees have felt the effects of what's called "Zoom fatigue," and companies are looking for better ways to engage employees online.

Through the metaverse, an online conference room will become much more realistic. The presentations will be more compelling, communication will feel more genuine, and the audience will be more engaged.

As metaverse workplaces prove to be useful, they could greatly increase the number of international teams. Furthermore, companies can hold their international meetings online and reduce their business travel expenses. Although the metaverse cannot completely replace human interaction, it can certainly speed it up. You can create a business that offers an international working hour scheduling service or create a translation plugin for international meetings. That is two excellent business models for the metaverse right there.

Gaming

Gaming will be one of the industries to cross the frontier into the metaverse. Virtual reality glasses caught the attention of the gaming industry when they were introduced. These days, popular game engines like Unity 3D offer developers to export their games for virtual reality. Moreover, 3D art and environments have been used in the industry for decades. We can expect game developers to be among the first to adapt to the upcoming metaverse.

They will be able to adapt quickly beyond the technical aspects of game development. Games with large followings, such as MMORPGs and MOBAs, have utilized their own currencies for in-game purchases for a long time. A few developers are now accepting cryptocurrency payments too.

The gaming industry has all these advantages over other industries, making it one of the poster children for Web 3.0. You can invest in the metaverse early on by investing in game studios that are shifting towards it. If you are a high-risk investor, look for angel investment opportunities in small startups. To be on the safe side, look for established game studios that are showing signs of making the shift. Collect stocks early and follow them regularly to ensure they are progressing.

Dating and Relationships

Online dating has changed the way we meet people many years ago. Nowadays, meeting someone is as simple as logging onto a website or downloading an app on your phone. We can only anticipate the metaverse to shake things up even more.

Remember that artificial intelligence and machine learning are crucial parts of Web 3.0. Dating applications like Tinder and OkCupid are wildly popular because they match us with people we're already interested in. This not only saves us time but increases the chances of a first date going well.

We can expect to see this on a larger scale once the metaverse starts influencing the dating world. Artificial intelligence will make smart guesses about our preferences. Whenever we express a liking or disliking for a specific trait, our choices will create a compound pool of characteristics we will be interested in.

We will be able to meet these people right away in the metaverse, which is even more exciting. Using this technology, we will be able to interact with people deeper without having to share personal information like phone numbers and addresses. This should make online dating a safer experience in the future.

Another group that will benefit from metaverse dating is long-distance couples. Some couples start off long-distance, and some evolve into long-distance relationships due to work like army officers. The metaverse era will give these people a chance to skip the Skype call and spend meaningful time with their loved ones.

Do you have a Christmas tradition of watching a certain holiday movie? Even when you are thousands of miles away from your loved ones, you can join the metaverse and watch the movie together. It doesn't end there. You can teach your children how to play chess, take your spouse on a two-hour date to Paris, and catch up with your friends on a virtual pick-up game. In the metaverse, you can do all of this and much more.

Media

Previously, we discussed the impact of information decentralization. One of the biggest industries to be affected by information decentralization was, undoubtedly, the mainstream media. Newspapers and news channels initially viewed the internet as a way to spread their accessibility. However, they took one of the biggest hits in the process.

Information democracy brought by the internet allows users to both generate and consume the information they want. Among the biggest reflections of this statement are the social media apps we use every day. Furthermore, the internet gives alternative media a fair chance to compete with mass media. As a result, the press no longer has a monopoly. A similar situation applies to big TV networks that have lost market share and influence to streaming services like Netflix.

It is hard to predict what Web 3.0 will bring to the table as far as the media is concerned. Web 3.0 is about us being able to see our input reflected back to us. Media outlets on the entertainment side might find it easier to adapt to Web 3.0. However, it remains unclear how the 24-hour news cycle will interact with Web 3.0. Governments will no doubt take action against the complete decentralization of news, as they do today. However, it can be speculated that self-journalism and social media will become more prominent. We will likely have more access to personal news stories that artificial intelligence thinks we will be interested in. In addition, there could be ways to set trigger alerts or mental health precautions based on what we consume. To date, Time has taken the boldest step into the metaverse from a media outlet. They are launching a weekly newsletter solely dedicated to the metaverse.

Education

The Covid-19 pandemic has proven that face-to-face education is not the only way to learn. While online education has its own challenges and setbacks, the metaverse can offer solutions. Using the metaverse, teachers can interact with children in virtual reality, which is a far cry from a Zoom call. Even more impressive, a teacher can instruct any student in any part of the world by means of machine learning techniques and translation technologies.

The metaverse has the potential to revolutionize education. Imagine yourself sitting in your Seattle home and taking a leisurely stroll in front of the Eiffel Tower with your favorite French teacher. Taking a school trip to Germany to learn about World War II without getting on a plane. Learn painting from Leonardo Da Vinci himself. Observing the human body from inside. These are a few examples of what virtual reality and artificial intelligence can do for the education system.

We can expect schools throughout the world to have metaverse campuses in the future. A few examples are already underway. A virtual campus will be created, for instance, at the Kenya-KAIST campus, which is expected to open by September 2023 in the Konza Technopolis. The University of Nicosia is preparing to open the first permanent university gallery for NFTs. They will also start offering a six-week course "Introduction to NFTs and the Metaverse," which starts in February 2022 as a part of their UNIC Open Metaverse Initiative. Over time, these examples will multiply and become more complex, resulting in student exchange programs being a daily occurrence.

Another group that will benefit from the educational implementation of the metaverse is students with disabilities. As a means of bridging the education gap between able-bodied and disabled students, augmented reality will be invaluable. It will be easier for teachers to design personalized activities for disabled students, and long-term hospitalization will not hinder academic success as much.

There is no doubt the metaverse will impact all industries one way or the other. What matters is how we respond to it. By embracing the metaverse early on and exploring its potential, we can take advantage of this wonderful technology and not let it pass us by as it changes the world.

12. A Step-By-Step Guide To Purchasing Real Estate In The Metaverse

Through a combination of augmented reality (AR), virtual reality (VR), and video, Metaverse is a step toward digitizing the actual world. Users can work, play, and communicate with pals in the virtual world using their digital avatars in the virtual universe. There are many things to do in the metaverse, from organizing a meeting to taking a virtual globe tour.

On the other hand, real estate appears to be capturing investors' attention. With unprecedented million-dollar purchases reported every other week, the volume of property deals in the metaverse has been making headlines.

To purchase virtual property, you must first register with a metaverse platform such as Decentraland, The Sandbox, or Axie Infinity, among others. Then, to transact in the metaverse, all you need is a well-funded digital wallet. Then, you can store your dollars in your digital wallet by converting them to cryptocurrencies like ether or native currencies of the metaverse you're transacting in, like MANA or Sandbox.

You may buy, rent, flip, or even sell homes in the digital world with the support of the metaverse's nearly full ecosystem, and ownership is based on non-fungible tokens (NFTs).

The following is a step-by-step guide to purchasing real estate in the metaverse.

1. Visit one of the metaverse's property marketplaces, such as Decentraland, Axie Infinity, or Sandbox, and log in.
2. Compare the prices of the various parcels of land that are available.
3. After you've chosen the digital plot of land you want to buy, click on it to learn more about it. It's vital to remember that a specific metaverse property platform will only enable you to buy from them if you use their approved cryptocurrency. Decentraland, for example, exclusively allows users to buy and sell homes with MANA, the company's cryptocurrency.
4. The next step is to connect your digital wallet to your account on the property site. To do so, you'll need to first obtain a suitable digital wallet. Metamask is the most popular digital wallet on the market right now. In addition, it's compatible with practically every metaverse property platform.

5. It's critical to fund your digital wallet with a cryptocurrency that works with the digital property platform you've chosen. Then, you may easily buy it on various exchanges and keep the cryptos safe in your digital wallet. All you have to do now is press the 'purchase' button when you've finished picking the land and funding your associated digital wallet.
6. Once you've completed the transaction, the digital land you've purchased is stored in your associated digital wallet as NFTs. So, in your digital wallet, go to the 'NFTs' page to see your newly bought land.

What you should know before buying metaverse real estate

Unlike investing in the real estate market, where your purchased physical land is guaranteed to survive, digital land in the metaverse will become non-existent if the platform you purchased fails and goes down. Another thing to remember is the significant volatility of the cryptocurrency used to transact in the metaverse's real estate market. Because the value of digital money fluctuates, the value of the metaverse property you possess fluctuates accordingly.

Furthermore, because digital real estate is a relatively new asset class, many facets have yet to be explored. As a result, investing in the metaverse's digital real estate market is very speculative; thus, thoroughly researching the advantages and downsides is recommended before making any decisions.

13. Ethics in the Metaverse

A major source of worry in the Metaverse is how to prevent toxicity or poor conduct in which people harass or intimidate others. Because many will be in the metaverse, it is obligatory upon its builders to make it a safe area for everybody. For example, people's opinions about sexuality might alter throughout time.

The difficulty had also evolved since, when we initially began with these internet experiences, whether virtualized or not, they did not incorporate as much of the actual world as they do now. The situation has changed. The Metaverse will soon be more like being in the actual world. We have to go through issues that no one else has gone through.

People will act if they see the metaverse as an add-on to reality rather than reality itself. Non-player characters may become more realistic, or perhaps smarter, in the future. According to Bartle, they may exhibit self-awareness. This might happen in the next few years, taking quantum computing to accomplish.

This poses a slew of ethical concerns. Are you going to eliminate the AI folks by erasing the database or turning it off? You might be able to resurrect them or at least duplicate them. Or do you destroy them by copying them? Have you become a mass killer if you develop a virtual environment for the sole purpose of killing characters?

You will then select the universe you want to visit, social or gaming realms. We will see a slew of small worlds or metaverses. A translation mechanism might be used to transport objects across Metaverse worlds.

You have to respect your players. Because you cannot leave the actual world if you do not like it, you will not be able to travel to another world where you do not have white hair. You have no choice but to remain in this reality. However, reality necessitates competition. You can always "go" to someone else's world if world operators surround you. You will have to respect them, or they will end up playing for someone else.

Simply, players want a place where they can be happy and be their best versions. In the physical world, the dice roll defines you. You do not have to be yourself in the virtual environment. You can uncover who you truly are. That is the kind of thing you would like to be able to see in the future.

Protocol Requirement Solution

With so many possibilities in the Metaverse, it is no surprise that so many technological behemoths continue to spend substantially on its growth. Because of the enormous potential influence, many people feel that this will be the next large-scale technology after the internet.

However, creating the "next internet" is easier said than done. Technical support for multiple dimensions and purposes, such as the ideal business economy, payment system, website economy, and other Web 3.0 aspects, is necessary to create the Metaverse.

As a Polkadot-based cross-chain protocol, X Protocol intends to fill this need. Polkadot (DOT) is a system that enables multiple blockchains to communicate similarly to the traditional internet by connecting different networks using Wanchain's decentralized bridges, a blockchain network interoperability framework. X Protocol thinks that by utilizing these elements, they will realize their goal of creating a "decentralized Metaverse based on Web 3.0."

To enter the Metaverse, the X Protocol Leverages Web 3.0. The protocol will establish a fair and decentralized standard for all economic activity while ensuring that any firm can freely distribute content. As a result, users may compare the X Protocol public chain to Ethereum (ETH), a blockchain well-known for its smart contract capabilities.

According to X Protocol, the focus has shifted to the basic layer one infrastructure, which comprises source-generated games and lands models. The project is written in RUST and revolves around the Polkadot and Solana (SOL) environment, comprising the protocol and application layers. The layers' major goals are to get organic traffic in the metaverse using self-developed decentralized apps (DApps) and give third-party DApps zero-barrier access to technological solutions.

X Protocol intends to produce DApps to attract organic users, then incorporate each DApp via Metaverse scenarios and give third-party DApps easy access to them; this will eventually result in a metaverse environment with a massive number of participants use cases. On Polkadot and Solana, X Protocol is rated one of the top metaverse projects in a group experience, linked wallets, and GitHub code volume.

On the X Protocol, a DeFi cross-chain asset pool is being constructed so that tokens generated on many blockchains may be freely exchanged irrespective of which chain they originate from. The X cross-chain bridge may be used to implement this swap capability on the platform. The X Protocol team believes that their approach will "significantly lower the transaction barrier" and "enhance the trading experience for users."

Conclusion

Suppose you are still trying to wrap your brain around virtual reality, augmented reality, mixed or extended reality ideas. In that case, it is time to move on because more tech firms are talking about a new era of the internet known as the Metaverse.

Despite its ambiguous definition, the word "Metaverse" is commonly used to express the idea of a future iteration of the internet consisting of shared, 3D virtual places linked into an imagined virtual world. In basic terms, the Metaverse is a virtual environment where you may use avatars to interact with other individuals in different geographical locations. Tech firms are considering various sorts of metaverse platforms. Users will buy land and develop ecosystems using NFTs and cryptocurrencies on a blockchain-based platform. A robust virtual environment where individuals may work, play, or interact could be another sort of platform. However, creating a Metaverse will rely heavily on AI and machine learning, as the metaverse's goal will be to combine our physical world with the virtual space via avatars. The Metaverse will be the convergence of virtual and augmented reality.

The Metaverse development will affect every facet of our civilization, especially entertainment, advertising, and the economy. The Metaverse, however, will have legal ramifications. Collaboration and interoperability between metaverse developers will be one concern. Intellectual property rights will be another issue, which is the case with most virtual products.

Even if the Metaverse currently falls short of the long-term vision that many have for it, it has the potential to alter how we interact with the virtual environment dramatically. A collaborative virtual experience, similar to NFTs, might open up new options for creators, gamers, entrepreneurs, investors, tech firms, and artists, not only restructuring but inventing the digital economy.

Whether it's a 2D web page or a 3D virtual world, the action of a widely recognized, representative, and authoritative organization to impose a reference standard with the participation of the main public and private stakeholders is essential. It is said that the meta-universe will belong to everyone, but at the same time, everyone is rushing to develop to seek a competitive advantage.

It should also be noted that the W3C era has undergone profound changes. Thirty years ago, it was in everyone's interest to create an environment that would allow new businesses to develop; no one would have thought that the Internet would get us where we are today, completely subverting social and economic patterns on a global scale.

The revolutionary momentum of the Internet has gradually given way to the dominance of large technology companies that occupy a strong position and are absolutely interested in creating new business platforms but will not risk losing the hegemony they enjoy. On the other hand, the government lags because technology continually works faster than regulatory design.

Aware of the risks and opportunities that will arise, it is necessary to find a basic condition of balance to make the metaverse a real development opportunity for all and the real manifestation of the dystopian scenarios described far.

Thank you for making it to the end of this book; we hope it has been informative and able to provide you with all the tools you need to achieve your goals, whatever they may be.

This book has tried to highlight all the important points so that you have a general and, in some cases, even specific knowledge about what will be the future of the Internet and all of society in the 21st century, so that you can benefit early from the future technological revolution while limiting its negative effects.

I hope this book will really help you achieve your goals.

www.ingramcontent.com/pod-product-compliance
Lightning Source LLC
LaVergne TN
LVHW082358200926
848481LV00012B/3608